Lecture Notes in Computer Science　14209

Founding Editors

Gerhard Goos
Juris Hartmanis

Editorial Board Members

The series Lecture Notes in Computer Science (LNCS), including its subseries Lecture Notes in Artificial Intelligence (LNAI) and Lecture Notes in Bioinformatics (LNBI), has established itself as a medium for the publication of new developments in computer science and information technology research, teaching, and education.

LNCS enjoys close cooperation with the computer science R & D community, the series counts many renowned academics among its volume editors and paper authors, and collaborates with prestigious societies. Its mission is to serve this international community by providing an invaluable service, mainly focused on the publication of conference and workshop proceedings and postproceedings. LNCS commenced publication in 1973.

Yuchao Zhang · Liang-Jie Zhang
Editors

Web Services – ICWS 2023

30th International Conference
Held as Part of the Services Conference Federation, SCF 2023
Honolulu, HI, USA, September 23–26, 2023
Proceedings

 Springer

Editors
Yuchao Zhang
Beijing University of Posts
and Telecommunications
Beijing, China

Liang-Jie Zhang ⓘ
Shenzhen Entrepreneurship and Innovation
Federation (SEIF)
Shenzhen, China

ISSN 0302-9743   ISSN 1611-3349 (electronic)
Lecture Notes in Computer Science
ISBN 978-3-031-44835-5   ISBN 978-3-031-44836-2 (eBook)
https://doi.org/10.1007/978-3-031-44836-2

This Springer imprint is published by the registered company Springer Nature Switzerland AG
The registered company address is: Gewerbestrasse 11, 6330 Cham, Switzerland

Paper in this product is recyclable.

Preface

The International Conference on Web Services (ICWS) is a prime international forum for both researchers and industry practitioners to exchange the latest fundamental advances in the state of the art and practice of Web-based services, identify emerging research topics, and define the future of Web-based services. All topics regarding Internet/Web services lifecycle study and management are aligned with the theme of ICWS.

ICWS 2023 was a member of the Services Conference Federation (SCF). SCF 2023 had the following 10 collocated service-oriented sister conferences: 2023 International Conference on Web Services (ICWS 2023), 2023 International Conference on Cloud Computing (CLOUD 2023), 2023 International Conference on Services Computing (SCC 2023), 2023 International Conference on Big Data (BigData 2023), 2023 International Conference on AI & Mobile Services (AIMS 2023), 2023 International Conference on Metaverse (METAVERSE 2023), 2023 International Conference on Internet of Things (ICIOT 2023), 2023 International Conference on Cognitive Computing (ICCC 2023), 2023 International Conference on Edge Computing (EDGE 2023), and 2023 International Conference on Blockchain (ICBC 2023).

This volume presents the accepted papers for the 2023 International Conference on Web Services (ICWS 2023), held during September 23–26, 2023. For this conference, each paper was single-blind reviewed by three independent members of the International Program Committee. After carefully evaluating their originality and quality, we have accepted 8 papers out of 14 submissions.

We are pleased to thank the authors whose submissions and participation made this conference possible. We also want to express our thanks to the Organizing Committee and Program Committee members, for their dedication in helping to organize the conference and reviewing the submissions. We owe special thanks to the keynote speakers for their impressive speeches.

Finally, we would like to thank operations team members Jing Zeng, Sheng He and Yishuang Ning for their excellent work in organizing this conference. We look forward to your future contributions as a volunteer, author, and conference participant in the fast-growing worldwide services innovations community.

September 2023   Yuchao Zhang
                                                                                                        Liang-Jie Zhang

Organization

Program Chair

Yuchao Zhang — Beijing University of Posts and Telecommunications, China

Services Conference Federation (SCF 2023)

General Chairs

Ali Arsanjani — Google, USA
Wu Chou — Essenlix Corporation, USA

Coordinating Program Chair

Liang-Jie Zhang — Shenzhen Entrepreneurship & Innovation Federation, China

CFO and International Affairs Chair

Min Luo — Georgia Tech, USA

Operation Committee

Jing Zeng — China Gridcom Co., Ltd., China
Yishuang Ning — Tsinghua University, China
Sheng He — Tsinghua University, China

Steering Committee

Calton Pu (Co-chair) — Georgia Tech, USA
Liang-Jie Zhang (Co-chair) — Shenzhen Entrepreneurship & Innovation Federation, China

ICWS 2023 Program Committee

Keke Gai	Beijing Institute of Technology, China
Hakim Hacid	Technology Innovation Institute, UAE
Dhaval Patel	IBM T. J. Watson Research Center, USA
Lei Yang	South China University of Technology, China
Haibo Zhang	University of Otago, New Zealand
Ikbal Taleb	Zayed University, UAE
Marios-Eleftherios Fokaefs	Polytechnique Montréal, Canada
Hyuk-Yoon Kwon	Seoul National University of Science & Technology, South Korea
Young-Kyoon Suh	Kyungpook National University, South Korea
Yuchao Zhang	Beijing University of Posts and Telecommunications, China

Conference Sponsor – Services Society

The Services Society (S2) is a non-profit professional organization that has been created to promote worldwide research and technical collaboration in services innovations among academia and industrial professionals. Its members are volunteers from industry and academia with common interests. S2 is registered in the USA as a "501(c) organization", which means that it is an American tax-exempt nonprofit organization. S2 collaborates with other professional organizations to sponsor or co-sponsor conferences and to promote an effective services curriculum in colleges and universities. S2 initiates and promotes a "Services University" program worldwide to bridge the gap between industrial needs and university instruction.

The Services Sector accounted for 79.5% of the GDP of the USA in 2016. The Services Society has formed 5 Special Interest Groups (SIGs) to support technology- and domain-specific professional activities.

- Special Interest Group on Services Computing (SIG-SC)
- Special Interest Group on Big Data (SIG-BD)
- Special Interest Group on Cloud Computing (SIG-CLOUD)
- Special Interest Group on Artificial Intelligence (SIG-AI)
- Special Interest Group on Metaverse (SIG-Metaverse)

About the Services Conference Federation (SCF)

As the founding member of the Services Conference Federation (SCF), the first **International Conference on Web Services (ICWS)** was held in June 2003 in Las Vegas, USA. Meanwhile, the First International Conference on Web Services - Europe 2003 (ICWS-Europe 2003) was held in Germany in October 2003. ICWS-Europe 2003 was an extended event of the 2003 International Conference on Web Services (ICWS 2003) in Europe. In 2004, ICWS-Europe was changed to the European Conference on Web Services (ECOWS), which was held at Erfurt, Germany. Sponsored by the Services Society and Springer, SCF 2018 and SCF 2019 were held successfully in Seattle and San Diego, USA. SCF 2020 and SCF 2021 were held successfully online and in Shenzhen, China. SCF 2022 was held successfully in Hawaii, USA. To celebrate its 21st birthday, SCF 2023 was held on September 23–26, 2023 in Honolulu Hawaii, USA with Satellite Sessions in Shenzhen, Guangdong, China and online.

In the past 20 years, the ICWS community has expanded from Web engineering innovations to scientific research for the whole services industry. Service delivery platforms have been expanded to mobile platforms, Internet of Things, cloud computing, and edge computing. The services ecosystem has gradually been enabled, value added, and intelligence embedded through enabling technologies such as big data, artificial intelligence, and cognitive computing. In the coming years, all transactions with multiple parties involved will be transformed to blockchain.

Based on technology trends and best practices in the field, the Services Conference Federation (SCF) will continue serving as the conference umbrella's code name for all services-related conferences. SCF 2023 defined the future of New ABCDE (AI, Blockchain, Cloud, BigData & IOT) and entered the 5G for Services Era. The theme of SCF 2023 was **Metaverse Era.** We are very proud to announce that SCF 2023's 10 co-located theme topic conferences all centered around "services", with each focusing on exploring different themes (web-based services, cloud-based services, Big Data-based services, services innovation lifecycle, AI-driven ubiquitous services, blockchain-driven trust service-ecosystems, industry-specific services and applications, and emerging service-oriented technologies).

- Bigger Platform: The 10 collocated conferences (SCF 2023) were sponsored by the Services Society, which is the world-leading not-for-profit organization (501 c(3)) dedicated for the service of more than 30,000 worldwide Services Computing researchers and practitioners. A bigger platform means bigger opportunities for all volunteers, authors, and participants. Meanwhile, Springer provided sponsorship to best paper awards and other professional activities. All the 10 conference proceedings of SCF 2023 were published by Springer and indexed in ISI Conference Proceedings Citation Index (included in Web of Science), Engineering Index EI (Compendex and Inspec databases), DBLP, Google Scholar, IO-Port, MathSciNet, Scopus, and ZBlMath.

- Brighter Future: While celebrating the 2023 version of ICWS, SCF 2023 highlighted the Second International Conference on Metaverse (METAVERSE 2023) to cover immersive services for all vertical industries and area solutions. It put its focus on the industry-specific services for digital transformation. This will lead our community members to create their own brighter future.
- Better Model: SCF 2023 continued to leverage the invented Conference Blockchain Model (CBM) to innovate the organizing practices for all the 10 theme conferences. Senior researchers in the field are welcome to submit proposals to serve as CBM Ambassador for an individual conference to start better interactions during your leadership role in for organizing future SCF conferences.

Contents

Research Track

A Multi-Armed Bandits Learning-Based Approach to Service Caching
in Edge Computing Environment 3
    Jinpeng Li, Jiale Zhao, Peng Chen, Yunni Xia, Fan Li, Yin Li,
    Feng Zeng, and Hui Liu

A Gap Between Automated Service Composition Research and Software
Engineering Development Practice: Service Descriptions 18
    Yang Syu and Chien-Min Wang

SPaMeR: Securing Patient Medical Records in the Cloud - A Microservice
and Brokerless Architecture Approach 32
    T. B. Nam, H. G. Khiem, M. N. Triet, K. V. Hong, T. D. Khoa, Q. T. Bao,
    N. T. Phuc, M. D. Hieu, V. C. P. Loc, T. L. Quy, N. T. Anh, Q. N. Hien,
    L. K. Bang, D. P. N. Trong, N. T. K. Ngan, H. Son, and H. H. Luong

Applying Blockchain Technology for Privacy Preservation in Android
Platforms 47
    H. G. Khiem, T. B. Nam, M. N. Triet, H. L. Huong, T. D. Khoa,
    Q. T. Bao, N. T. Phuc, M. D. Hieu, V. C. P. Loc, T. L. Quy, N. T. Anh,
    Q. N. Hien, L. K. Bang, D. P. N. Trong, N. T. K. Ngan, H. Son,
    and K. V. Hong

Application and Industry Track

A Semi-supervised Learning Based Method for Identifying Idle Virtual
Machines in Managed Cloud: Application and Practice 65
    Xian Yu, Kejiang Ye, Zihong Chen, Jia Yi, Xiaofan Chen, Bozhong Liu,
    and Chengzhong Xu

MyKSC: Disaggregated Containerized Supercomputer Platform 83
    Ju-Won Park, Joon Woo, and Taeyoung Hong

Research on Network Slicing Deployment Strategy for High Reliability
Power Business Service 92
    Jinyu Zhao, Lin Pang, Jiayi Liu, and Dalong Song

Short Paper Track

An In-Depth Examination of Ultra-Wide Band (UWB) Pulse Duration
for Accurate Localization 107
  Somayeh Mohammady

Author Index 121

Research Track

A Multi-Armed Bandits Learning-Based Approach to Service Caching in Edge Computing Environment

Jinpeng Li[1], Jiale Zhao[1](✉), Peng Chen[2], Yunni Xia[1](✉), Fan Li[3], Yin Li[4], Feng Zeng[5], and Hui Liu[6]

[1] School of Computer, Chongqing University, Chongqing 400030, China
zhaojiale0415@163.com, xiayunni@hotmail.com
[2] School of Computer and Software Engineering, Xihua University,
Chengdu 610039, China
[3] Key Laboratory of Fundamental Synthetic Vision Graphics and Image Science for
National Defense, Sichuan University, Chengdu 610065, China
[4] Guangzhou Institute of Software Application Technology, Guangzhou 510990,
China
[5] Discovery Technology (Shenzhen)Limited, Shenzhen 518129, China
[6] School of Computer Science and Technology, Beijing Institute of Technology,
Beijing 100083, China

Abstract. Mobile edge computing (MEC) is a newly emerging concept that provides significant local computing power and reduces end-to-end latency. In MEC environments, caching frequently accessed services on edge servers effectively reduces latency and improves system responsiveness. An ongoing research topic in such a cachable MEC context is to design novel algorithms for yielding high-quality caching decision that guarantee high user-perceived quality-of-service (QoS) and high system responsiveness of delivery of cached content with the difference of caching capacities of edge servers and diversified content popularity appropriately addressed. In this article, we propose a multi-armed bandits learning-based method busing a Thompson sampling for generating caching decisions. We introduce a genetic multi-armed bandits algorithm (GMAB), which synthesizes the genetic algorithm (GA) and multi-armed bandits (MAB), for optimizing caching effectiveness with timing and space constraints. The experiment results show that GMAB outperforms traditional methods in terms of multiple aspects.

Keywords: Edge computing · Multi-armed bandits learning · Service caching · Thompson sampling · Genetic algorithm

1 Introduction

The world today is witnessing a rapid growth in the number of smart Internet-of-Things (IoT) devices including mobile phones, smart watches, mobile computers and autonomous cars [1]. These devices introduce massive data computing requirements, especially for delay-sensitive services, which brings great

Y. Zhang and L.-J. Zhang (Eds.): ICWS 2023, LNCS 14209, pp. 3–17, 2023.
https://doi.org/10.1007/978-3-031-44836-2_1

challenges to the mobile cloud computing (MCC). In a traditional centralized environment, computation-demanding tasks are offloaded to the resource-rich cloud center, resulting in significant contents transmission delays for sending and receiving data from IoT to the cloud, which seriously affects efficiency of content delivery. MEC enables intelligent content caching at the network edge to reduce traffic and enhance content delivery efficiency. In MEC architecture, popular content can be deployed at the MEC server to improve users' quality of experience (QoE). The edge servers with a certain cache of computing resources are attached to base stations or access points close to users, providing users with real-time computing and data storage services at the edge of network. In the MEC environment, tasks can be offloaded from IoT devices to the optimal edge servers to avoid data transmission from the cloud.

Despite its benefits, caching at MEC faces several challenges, such as unpredictable user mobility, limited storage space of edge nodes, and unpredictability of content requests. One critical challenge is to achieve good tradeoffs among efficiency of content delivery (in terms of, e.g., cache hit rate and response time) and system overhead (in terms of, e.g., backhaul traffic).

In this study, we propose a genetic multi-armed bandits (GMAB) learning-based method to yielding dynamic service caching schemes in MEC, the main contributions are as follows:

1) We design a decentralized decision-making mechanism, where each edge server runs a GMAB in a decentralized manner.
2) We accelerate convergence speed by leveraging a genetic reinforcement learning algorithm, which is capable of adapting caching schemes to real-time changes of task types.
3) To evaluate the performance of GMAB, we conduct extensive simulations by using a real-world data set and show that our proposed method outperforms its peers in terms of multiple performance indicators.

This paper is organized as follows: In Sect. 2, we review some related work. The system models and problem definition are given in Sect. 3. The proposed method is described in Sect. 4, and performance evaluation is presented in Sect. 5.

2   Related Work

Caching data on the edge server, which is near the user, is a evolving technique used in various areas. In recent years, it has attracted many researchers' attention as an active research topic.

Least Recently Used (LRU) and Least Recently Visited (LFU) are the two most used strategies in this direction [2,3]. Xia et al. [4] provided an online algorithm for the collaborative problem in MEC environment by modeling the edge caching problem as a constrained optimization matter. Zhao et al. [5] introduced a service placement method over vehicular to address the challenge of improving the caching hit rate. Zeng et al. [6] integrated user behavioral preferences and contextual zoom to develop a heuristic intelligent caching scheme. The objective is to optimize the priority content under the historical request count of the corresponding content.

Recently, machine learning models and algorithms showed their ability in yielding and optimizing MEC caching schemes. Sengupta et al. [7] addressed the distributed caching problem in mobile edge networks from the perspective of reinforcement learning. Zhong et al. [8] proposed an actor-critic (AC) learning framework to optimize content delivery latency. Song et al. [9] studied the collaborative shared cache problem of static users in the MEC environment, modeled a single agent learning mechanism for optimizing caching decisions. Wu et al. [10] formulate the resource allocation strategy as a joint optimization problem, and they use deep Q-learning network (DQN) for solving this problem. Recently, the shortcoming of DQN has also gained considerable deliberation because of the difficulties in handing a large action space. Qiao et al. [11] proposed a cooperative edge caching scheme suitable for complicated action space relying on a deep deterministic policy gradient (DDPG) model.

Multi-armed bandits (MAB)-based methods is frequently seen in this direction as well. Malazi et al. [12] proposed a distributed caching strategy that describes the edge service placement problem as a multi-armed bandit problem and used the upper confidence bound (UCB1) algorithm for optimization. Wu et al. [13] considered MEC caching mechanisms over multi-rat heterogeneous networks and extracted the parts that can be measured in real-time when they used UCB1 to calculate rewards for reducing the workload. Chen et al. [14] studied the spatial-temporal edge service caching problem of an application service providers under a limited budget and proposed an contextual bandit learning algorithm to optimize the edge computing performance. Xu et al. [15] proposed a collaborative cache management algorithm that maximizes cache service traffic while minimizing bandwidth costs. Jiang et al. [16] studied a collaboration scheme between MEC servers to optimize content caching and delivery performance between MEC and mobile devices. Ren et al. [17,18] proposed a grouping-based caching strategy and considered allocating storage resources to reduce the average latency and total energy consumption in content retrieval.

3   System Models and Problem Formulation

3.1   System Model

In this article, we consider a MEC environment built upon a remote cloud and a set of base stations equipped with edge servers linked to the cloud through a backhaul network. As shown in Fig. 1, our caching model is built upon the MEC environment and it comprises a task offloading model and a service cache model. When a task request reaches the edge server, it can only be executed if the corresponding type of service is cached there. Our aim is thus to optimize the schedules for updating the service cache with satisfactory performance.

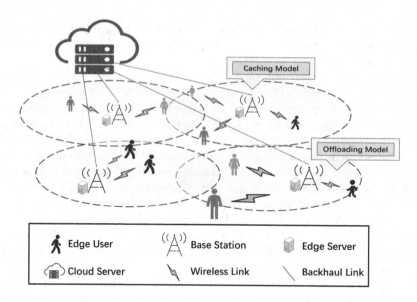

Fig. 1. Edge computing system model.

   The central cloud is capable of handling all types of tasks and c_c^i is the capacity for service s_i in the cloud. $E = \{e_1, e_2, ..., e_m\}$ denotes the set of edge servers deployed in the current area. Each edge server can be described by a 5-tuple $e_i = (L_i, r_i, b_i, C_i, N_i)$, where $L_i = (lot, lat)$ denotes the geographical position of e_i, r_i the radius of its signal coverage, b_i the capacity of caching services for e_i, $C_i = \{c_i^1, c_i^2, ..., c_i^n\}$ a set of the ability to handle tasks, c_i^j the computational capacity of edge server e_i for task k_j and $N_i = \{e_{i_1}, e_{i_2}, ..., e_{i_s}\}$ the set of neighboring and wireless network-reachable servers of e_i. $S = \{s_1, s_2, ..., s_k\}$ is defined as the set of all services. $K(t) = \{k_1, k_2, ..., k_n\}$ denotes the set of all tasks for e_i at time t. Each task can be described by a 4-tuple $k_j = (q_j, s_l, d_j, p_j)$, where q_j denotes the location of task k_j, s_l the required service type by task k_j, d_j the up-link data size and p_j the computational overhead. A user and a base stations are connected with Standalone (SA) or Non-Standalone Access (NSA) 5G network. Base stations themselves are inter-connected via X2 or Xn links [19]. $W_e(t)$ denotes the bandwidth of 5G at time t, and $W_c(t)$ the bandwidth of the inter edge-cloud backbone network at time t. All symbols appearing in this paper are shown in Table 1.

Table 1. Notion table

Variable	Description
c_c^i	The capacity for handling s_i in the cloud
E	A set of edge servers
e_i	The i-th edge server
L_i	The geographical position of e_i
r_i	The signal radius of e_i
b_i	The capacity of caching services for e_i
C_i	A set of the ability of e_i to handle tasks
N_i	A set of neighboring and wireless network-reachable servers of e_i
S	A set of all services
$K(t)$	A set of all tasks for e_i at time t
k_j	The j-th task in K^t
q_j	The location of k_j
s_l	The required service by k_j
d_j	The up-link data size of k_j
p_j	The computational overhead of k_j
$W_e(t)$	The bandwidth of 5G at time t
$W_c(t)$	The bandwidth of the inter edge-cloud backbone network at time t
$y_{i,j}(t)$	A binary variable showing whether the service sj is cached in e_i at time t
$q(s_j)$	The data size of s_j
$tcor_{i,j}(t)$	The transmission time when k_j is offloaded to e_i and no malfunctioning
$terr_{i,j}(t)$	The transmission time when k_j is offloaded to e_i and failure occurs
$tt_{i,j}(t,u)$	The transmission time between k_j to e_i
$tc_{i,j}(t)$	The calculation delay of the k_j
$ra_i(t)$	The average hit rate of e_i

3.2 Service Caching Model

Due to limited storage and computing capacity, edge servers can only cache a portion of services and thus cached content is updatable and replaceable. A binary variable $y_{i,j}(t)$ denotes whether the service s_j is cached in e_i at time t according to (1).

$$y_{i,t}(t) = \begin{cases} 1, \text{ if } s_j \text{ is cached in } e_i \\ 0, \text{ otherwise} \end{cases} \tag{1}$$

Instead of using traditional virtual machines, we consider that the caching system is empowered by containerization technologies (e.g., Docker), which can reduce cache costs and improve service utilization by enabling quick adaptation to request pattern variability. The maximum number of storage services for edge servers is limited by the container size according to (2). (2) implies that a service s_d can be cached in e_i at time t when the corresponding container size is sufficient.

$$\sum_{j=1,j\neq d}^{k} (y_{i,j}(t) \cdot q(s_j)) + q(s_d) \leq b_i \tag{2}$$

where $q(s_j)$ denotes the data size of s_j.

3.3 Task Offloading Model

Task offloading model specifies how tasks are allocated for requesting cached content nearby. Each user can only be connected to one edge server e_i at a time. When receiving a request k_j, which requires service s_l to be processed, edge server e_i checks the availability of requested content. If e_i fails to hit s_l, this request is forwarded to the neighboring server N_i. When both e_i and N_i fail to offer s_i, the request is forwarded to the cloud. In addition, we assume that content delivery can fail, e.g., unstable wireless connection. In case of failure, e_i forwards k_j to the cloud as well. (3) specifies the transmission delay under different conditions when k_j is offloaded to e_i and the edge server is not malfunctioning.

$$tcor_{i,j}(t) = \begin{cases} \frac{d_j}{W_e(t)\log_2(1+\frac{\rho_j\tau_{ij}}{\lambda^2})}, & (y_{i,l}(t) = 1) \\ \frac{2d_j}{W_e(t)\log_2(1+\frac{\rho_j\tau_{Nij}}{\lambda^2})}, & (y_{i,l}(t) = 0)\&(\exists y_{Ni,l}(t) = 1) \\ \frac{d_j}{W_e(t)\log_2(1+\frac{\rho_j\tau_{cj}}{\lambda^2})}, & \text{otherwise} \end{cases} \tag{3}$$

where ρ_j denotes the transmission power of user devices, τ_{ij} the channel gain between the device requesting k_j and e_i, τ_{cj} the channel gain between the device requesting k_j and $cloud$ and λ^2 the background noise power. If failure occurs, e_i forwards k_j to the cloud and the transmission delay of e_i is:

$$terr_{i,j}(t) = \begin{cases} tcor_{i,j}(t) + \frac{d_j}{W_e(t)\log_2(1+\frac{\rho_j\tau_{cj}}{\lambda^2})}, & (y_{i,l}(t) = 1) \\ tcor_{i,j}(t) + \frac{d_j}{W_e(t)\log_2(1+\frac{\rho_j\tau_{Ncj}}{\lambda^2})}, & (y_{i,l}(t) = 0)\&(\exists y_{Ni,l}(t) = 1) \\ tcor_{i,j}(t), & \text{otherwise} \end{cases} \tag{4}$$

Therefore, the transmission time between user to e_i for offloading k_j at t is:

$$tt_{i,j}(t,u) = u \cdot terr_{i,j}(t) + (1-u) \cdot tcor_{i,j}(t) \tag{5}$$

where u is the error rate of edge servers, $terr_{i,j}(t)$ and $tcor_{i,j}(t)$ are defined in (3) and (4) respectively. The calculation delay of the k_j is represented by (6), and the average hit rate of e_i is defined as (7).

The calculation delay $tc_{i,j}(t)$ is determined by the computational overhead and the capacity for handling tasks, and the hit rate $ra_i(t)$ is the ratio of the number of tasks hit on the edge side to the total number of tasks.

$$tc_{i,j}(t) = \beta_{i,j}(t) \cdot \frac{p_j}{c_i^l} + (1 - \beta_{i,j}(t)) \cdot \frac{p_j}{c_c^l} \tag{6}$$

$$ra_i(t) = \frac{\sum_{j=1}^{n}(\beta_{i,j}(t) + \beta_{N_i,j}(t))}{n} \tag{7}$$

where $\beta_{i,j}(t)$ is a boolean indicator of whether k_j is executed at e_i, and n is the number of elements in $K(t)$, which represents the total number of tasks accessing e_i at time t.

3.4   Problem Formulation

In the MEC environment, edge servers can cache only a portion of services as mentioned earlier. Given the system model described above, our goals are as follows:

1. Minimize the average response delays according to (8).
2. Maximize hit rate according to (9).

$$\text{Min} : \frac{1}{n} \sum_{i=1}^{m} \sum_{j=1}^{n} \sum_{t=0}^{t_{max}} (tt_{i,j}(t,u) + tc_{i,j}(t)) \tag{8}$$

$$\text{Max} : \sum_{i=1}^{m} \sum_{t=0}^{t_{max}} ra_i(t) \tag{9}$$

$$s.t. \quad \textbf{C1.} \quad \sum_{j=1}^{k} y_{i,j}(t) < b_i \qquad \forall i, \forall t$$

$$\textbf{C2.} \quad \sqrt{(q_j - Li)^2} < r_i \quad \forall i, \forall j, \forall t$$

$C1$ indicates the size of the stored services is bounded by the caching size of the edge server. $C2$ represents the data transmission between edge servers and users occurs within the radius of the e_i signal coverage.

The above formulation can be considered as a capacitated facility location problem (CFLP) with a set of facilities (edge servers) and a set of customers (users). Facilities have a caching capacity, and their establishment process is similar to caching a service. Building a facility has the same cost as caching a service. The serving cost of customers includes both the service response time and the hit rate. The objective is to build facilities with constraints to minimize customer service costs. CFLP is NP-hard [20] and thus (8–9) is also an NP-hard as well.

4   The Proposed Method

This section outlines the genetic multi-armed bandits (GMAB) for yielding high-quality solutions to the formulation given above. The real-time service caching problem can be interpreted as a multi-armed bandits problem with n unknown and independent bonus probability distributions. Each edge server operates a multi-armed bandits algorithm where each arm represents a different service. Selecting an arm is equivalent to caching a service and an edge server periodically evaluates the current policy, as well as making caching replacements. An edge server selects multiple arms during each decision round based on the highest expected reward and the current caching state.

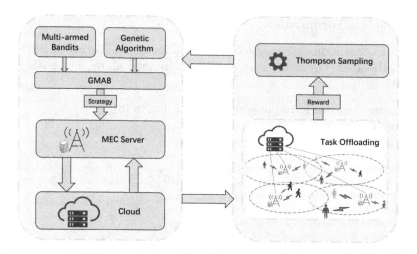

Fig. 2. Framework of GMAB for yielding the caching strategy.

As shown in Fig. 2, the bandit mechanism is deployed on each MEC server and it generates a new caching strategy for each time epoch to update the cache content from the cloud. The MEC environment generates a reward for the current strategy at each time epoch and provides feedbacks to Thompson Sampling, which ultimately determines the caching strategy for the next epoch.

4.1 Genetic Multi-armed Bandits Algorithm

At every epoch (with input T), Algorithm 1 determines if a caching update is necessary (Line 3). When an update is required, Q_{max} and R_{max} are checked for updates (Lines 4–7). The Bandit mechanism takes a new reward from $beta(\alpha, \beta)$ (Line 9) and searches for a new caching queue based on the reward through: 1) selecting the services with the largest reward to Q_2 (Lines 13–15); 2) shifting the focus to the uncached remaining services (Lines 17–20) for delayed opportunities of being selected. A genetic algorithm is used as well to cross Q_2 and Q_{max} for an improved convergence (Line 21). Finally, the MEC server caches the services that are placed in Q_2 and notifies its neighbors(Line 22). R is updated every epoch (Line 25). The modified genetic algorithm and the task offloading algorithm are discussed in Sect. 4.2 and 4.3, respectively.

Algorithm 1: Genetic Multi-armed Bandits Algorithm

Input: time interval T, tasks of users K, MEC server e_i, application services S

1 **Initialize** beta distribution $b(\alpha, \beta)$, current optimal strategy Q_{max}, caching reward R

2 **foreach** *episode* **do**

3   **if** $t \bmod T == 0$ **then**

4   **if** $R > R_{max}$ **then**

5             $Q_{max} \leftarrow Q_2$

6             $R_{max} \leftarrow R$

7   **end**

8         $R \leftarrow 0$

9   **foreach** $s \in S$ **do**

10   Sampling reward value R_s from $b(\alpha, \beta)$

11   **end**

12         $Q_1 \leftarrow$ Sort services in descending order of R

13         $Q_2 \leftarrow \emptyset, c \leftarrow 0$

14   **while** $c < \frac{e_i[2]}{2}$ **do**

15   Select the service s_c with the highest R from Q_1 to place in Q2 and remove s_c from Q1 $c \leftarrow c + 1$

16   **end**

17         $c \leftarrow 0$

18   **while** $c < \frac{e_i[2]}{2}$ **do**

19   Select the uncached service s_c with the highest R from Q_1 to place in Q2 and remove s_c from Q1

20             $c \leftarrow c + 1$

21   **end**

22   Genetic_crossover()

23   Cache Q_2 into the server and synchronize information from adjacent servers

24   **end**

25     $R_q \leftarrow$ Environment_interaction()

26     $R \leftarrow R + R_q$

27 **end**

4.2 Modified Genetic Algorithm

As mentioned earlier, a modified genetic algorithm is incorporated for improving the convergence. As shown in Algorithm 2, it: 1) extracts services that are in Q_2 but not in Q_{max} (Lines 2–6); 2) extracts services that are in Q_{max} but not in Q_2 (Lines 7–11) and 3) puts them into S_1 and S_2.

Algorithm 2: Modified Genetic Algorithm

Input: services list Q_2, pre-optimal strategy Q_{max}
1 **Initialize** $S_1 \leftarrow \emptyset$, $S_2 \leftarrow \emptyset$
2 **foreach** $q \in Q_2$ **do**
3   **if** $q \notin Q_{max}$ **then**
4   Put q into S_1
5   **end**
6 **end**
7 **foreach** $q \in Q_{max}$ **do**
8   **if** $q \notin Q_2$ **then**
9   Put q into S_2
10   **end**
11 **end**
12 **foreach** $s \in S_2$ **do**
13      $a \leftarrow Random()$
14   **if** $a < 0.1$ **then**
15   Remove $S_1[0]$ form Q_2
16   Remove $S_1[0]$ form S_1
17          $Q_2 \leftarrow Q_2 \cup \{s\}$
18   **end**
19 **end**
20 **return** Q_2

4.3 Task Offloading Algorithm

We provided a detailed introduction of the task offloading process in Algorithm 3. When a task request arrives, the edge node e_i that is connected to the user, the neighbor N_{e_i} or the cloud can all respond and provide the required computing services. If e_i fails to hit the cache, this request is forwarded to N_{e_i} (Lines 2–7). When both e_i and N_{e_i} fail to hit or some errors occur on the edge side, the request is forwarded to the cloud (Lines 8–11). After all tasks are completed at the current time, the reward value R_s will be calculated by (10), and $b(\alpha, \beta)$ will be updated according to (11) (Lines 14–16). Finally, the reward value Rq of the caching strategy is calculated by (12) and returned to GMAB along with $b(\alpha, \beta)$(Lines 18-19).

$$R_i = \frac{n_{s_i}}{n_{max}} \cdot \left(\frac{k \cdot o_{s_i}}{\sum_{j=1}^{k} o_{s_j}} + \frac{k \cdot d_{s_i}}{\sum_{j=1}^{k} d_{s_j}} \right) \tag{10}$$

where n_{s_i} and n_{max} are the times of requesting service s_i and the max times in all services, respectively, o_{s_i} the average latency sensitivity of all tasks that requesting s_i and d_{s_i} the average up-link data size of all tasks that requesting s_i.

$$b(\alpha, \beta) = \begin{cases} b(\alpha + 1, \beta), & (R_{ss} = 1) \\ b(\alpha, \beta + 1), & (R_{ss} = 0) \end{cases} \tag{11}$$

Algorithm 3: Task Offloading Algorithm

Input: tasks of users K_t, application services S

1 **foreach** $k \in K_t$ **do**
2   **if** *the required services for k are cached in server* e_i **then**
3 | forward k to e_i
4   **end**
5   **else if** *the required services for k are cached in server* $e_j \in N_{e_i}$ **then**
6 | forward k to e_j
7   **end**
8   **else**
9 | forward k to cloud
10   **end**
11   If the error occurs at the edge, the task will be forwarded to the cloud.
12 **end**
13 **foreach** $s \in S$ **do**
14   calculate reward R_s for service s according to (10)
15   map R_s to R_{ss} which can only be number 0 or 1
16   update parameters for $b(\alpha, \beta)$ according to (11)
17 **end**
18 calculate reward R_q for current strategy according to (12)
19 **return** $R_q, b(\alpha, \beta)$

$$R_q = \sum_{j=1}^{k} (y_{i,j}^t \cdot R_i \cdot \frac{u_j}{b_i}) \tag{12}$$

where u_j is the size of s_j.

5 Performance Evaluation

We build a real-world simulation environment based on the Shanghai Telecom's base station data set, which contains 7.2 million internet access logs from 3,233 edge stations for 9,481 mobile users over 6 months. If a user has access to the internet, we can know when it sends a request and which base station the user is connected to. Figure 3 shows the distribution of nodes on the edge of Shanghai. We use Python to implement the proposed method. Chen *et al.* reported the round-trip time to the public cloud is 74 milliseconds, which we also used in our evaluation. We set the task's error rate at the edge to 1% and check for updates to caching every 5 epochs. To study the effect of the modified genetic algorithm, we design an experiment to compare the convergence speed of the algorithm, with and without the modified genetic algorithm. The parameters related to the simulation are shown in Table 2.

All the experiments are conducted on the same computer with an AMD Ryzen7 6800H 3.20 GHz processor, 16.0 GB of RAM, and using Python 3.10.

Table 2. Parameter table

Parameters	Value
Type of requests	800
Caching size of edge servers	0–450
Up-link data size(MB)	0.5–50
Channel bandwidth between edge servers(MHz)	20
Channel bandwidth between edge servers and cloud(MHz)	500
Signal transmission power(W)	0.5
Channel gain	$[D(e_i, r_j)]^4$
Computing amount of tasks(TFLOPs)	1.2-3.6
Computing capability of edge servers(TFLOPS)	0.4–1.2
Total rounds of simulation	500

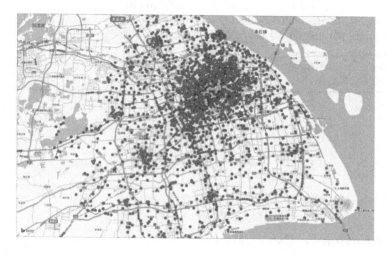

Fig. 3. Distribution of all 3,233 base stations in Shanghai. Each node denotes a base station.

We compared the performance of our proposed method with four baselines. We consider using the Oracle method as the first baseline, which possesses complete and accurate information about future service requests (i.e. has sufficient knowledge about future task types). This baseline is used to evaluate the effectiveness of our proposed methods in adapting to future changes in service requirements. The second baseline is the DCC-MAB algorithm proposed by Malazi *et al.* [12], which uses a modified UCB1 method to drive the bandit algorithm. The third method is based on the centralized multi-armed bandit method introduced by Chen *et al.* [14]. This method allows for the placement of each service in a fixed number of edge servers to meet budget constraints. The last baseline is the distributed collaborative service placement method presented in Yu *et al.* [21].

Figure 4 shows the caching hit rates of different strategies under different caching capacities of the MEC servers. It is obvious that the caching hit rate increases with increasing MEC server capacity. The Oracle method performs 2% higher than GMAB, while GMAB beats DCC-MAB/Chen *et al.*/Yu *et al.* by 5.2%/6.3%/ 11.1%, respectively.

Figure 5 reveals that our proposed method has made significant improvement in response latency. The average response time of the Oracle method is 4% lower than GMAB, while GMAB produces an average response time that is 2% lower than that of the DCC-MAB method, and is 5.4%/15.6% lower than Chen *et al.*/Yu *et al.*, respectively.

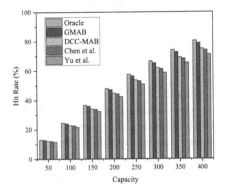

Fig. 4. Capacity and Hit Rate.   **Fig. 5.** Capacity and Response Time.

Figure 6 shows that the backhaul traffic of different algorithms shows a decreasing trend with the increase of caching capacity. The proposed GMAB approach has a backhaul traffic reduction of 7.1% compared to the baseline Oracle. The GMAB achieves the best performance in comparison with the other algorithms. Specifically, the backhaul traffic of GMAB averages 3.1% lower than DCC-MAB, 14.9% lower than that of Chen *et al.*, and 44.5% lower than that of Yu *et al.*.

Furthermore, we design an experiment to analyze the effectiveness of the modified genetic algorithm for MAB. The O-MAB refers to the GMAB method lacking the modified genetic algorithm. The plot in Fig. 7 illustrates that, despite the fact that both O-MAB and GMAB achieved the same hit rate eventually, the convergence speed of O-MAB was substantially lower than that of GMAB. Moreover, DCC-MAB performed even worse than O-MAB in terms of both convergence speed and hit rate.

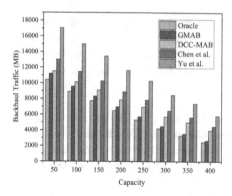
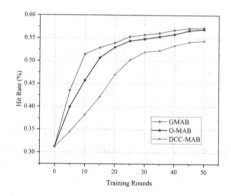

Fig. 6. Capacity and Backhaul Traffic.   **Fig. 7.** Training Rounds and Hit Rate.

6 Conclusion

In this paper, we study the service caching problem in an MEC environment and present a Multi-Armed Bandits Learning-based caching method, GMAB. It comprises a genetic multi-armed bandits model for yielding high-quality caching schedules and a genetic algorithms for optimizing the convergence speed. The experimental results obtained upon a real-world date set of Shanghai Telecom's base station demonstrate that GMAB outperforms its peers in terms of multiple performance aspects.

References

1. Xu, X., Chen, P., Xia, Y., Long, M., Peng, Q., Long, T.: Mroco: a novel approach to structured application scheduling with a hybrid vehicular cloud-edge environment, in. IEEE Int. Conf. Serv. Comput. (SCC) **2022**, 84–92 (2022)
2. Ioannou, A., Weber, S.: A survey of caching policies and forwarding mechanisms in information-centric networking. IEEE Commun. Surv. Tutorials **18**(4), 2847–2886 (2016)
3. Ahlehagh, H., Dey, S.: Video caching in radio access network: impact on delay and capacity, in. IEEE Wirel. Commun. Network. Conf. (WCNC) **2012**, 2276–2281 (2012)
4. Xia, X., Chen, F., He, Q., Grundy, J., Abdelrazek, M., Jin, H.: Online collaborative data caching in edge computing. IEEE Trans. Parallel Distrib. Syst. **32**(2), 281–294 (2021)
5. Zhao, J., Sun, X., Li, Q., Ma, X.: Edge caching and computation management for real-time internet of vehicles: an online and distributed approach. IEEE Trans. Intell. Transp. Syst. **22**(4), 2183–2197 (2021)
6. Zeng, Y., et al.: Smart caching based on user behavior for mobile edge computing. Inf. Sci. **503**, 444–468 (2019)

7. Sengupta, A., Amuru, S., Tandon, R., Buehrer, R.M., Clancy, T.C., Learning distributed caching strategies in small cell networks. In: 11th International Symposium on Wireless Communications Systems (ISWCS). IEEE 2014, pp. 917–921 (2014)

8. Zhong, C., Gursoy, M.C., Velipasalar, S.: Deep reinforcement learning-based edge caching in wireless networks. IEEE Trans. Cogn. Commun. Network. **6**(1), 48–61 (2020)

9. Song, J., Sheng, M., Quek, T.Q., Xu, C., Wang, X.: Learning-based content caching and sharing for wireless networks. IEEE Trans. Commun. **65**(10), 4309–4324 (2017)

10. Wu, P., Li, J., Shi, L., Ding, M., Cai, K., Yang, F.: Dynamic content update for wireless edge caching via deep reinforcement learning. IEEE Commun. Lett. **23**(10), 1773–1777 (2019)

11. Qiao, G., Leng, S., Maharjan, S., Zhang, Y., Ansari, N.: Deep reinforcement learning for cooperative content caching in vehicular edge computing and networks. IEEE Internet Things J. **7**(1), 247–257 (2020)

12. Malazi, H.T., Clarke, S.: Distributed service placement and workload orchestration in a multi-access edge computing environment. IEEE Int. Conf. Serv. Comput. (SCC) **2021**, 241–251 (2021)

13. Wu, B., Chen, T., Yang, K., Wang, X.: Edge-centric bandit learning for task-offloading allocations in multi-rat heterogeneous networks. IEEE Trans. Veh. Technol. **70**(4), 3702–3714 (2021)

14. Chen, L., Xu, J., Ren, S., Zhou, P.: Spatio-temporal edge service placement: a bandit learning approach. IEEE Trans. Wireless Commun. **17**(12), 8388–8401 (2018)

15. Xu, H., Chen, R., Xu, M., Jiang, M., Lu, X.: Device-to-device collaborative caching strategy based on incentive mechanism. IEEE/CIC Int. Conf. Commun. China (ICCC) **2021**, 612–617 (2021)

16. Jiang, W., Feng, G., Qin, S.: Optimal cooperative content caching and delivery policy for heterogeneous cellular networks. IEEE Trans. Mob. Comput. **16**(5), 1382–1393 (2017)

17. Ren, D., Gui, X., Lu, W., An, J., Dai, H., Liang, X.: Ghcc: grouping-based and hierarchical collaborative caching for mobile edge computing. In: 16th International Symposium on Modeling and Optimization in Mobile, Ad Hoc, and Wireless Networks (WiOpt). IEEE, pp. 1–6 (2018)

18. Ren, D., et al.: Hierarchical resource distribution network based on mobile edge computing, in 2017 IEEE 23rd International Conference on Parallel and Distributed Systems (ICPADS). IEEE, 2017, pp. 57–64 (2017)

19. Lin, X., et al.: 5G new radio: unveiling the essentials of the next generation wireless access technology. IEEE Commun. Standards Mag. **3**(3), 30–37 (2019). https://doi.org/10.1109/MCOMSTD.001.1800036

20. Wu, L.Y., Zhang, X.S., Zhang, J.L.: Capacitated facility location problem with general setup cost. Comput. Oper. Res., vol. 33, pp. 1226–1241, 2006. https://doi.org/10.1016/j.cor.2004.09.012

21. Yu, N., Xie, Q., Wang, Q., Du, H., Huang, H., Jia, X.: Collaborative service placement for mobile edge computing applications. In: IEEE Global Communications Conference, GLOBECOM 2018, Abu Dhabi, United Arab Emirates, December 9–13, 2018. IEEE, 2018, pp. 1–6. https://doi.org/10.1109/GLOCOM.2018.8647338

A Gap Between Automated Service Composition Research and Software Engineering Development Practice: Service Descriptions

Yang Syu[1,2]([⊠]) and Chien-Min Wang[2]

[1] Department of Information Science, National Taipei University of Education, Taipei City,
Taiwan (R.O.C.)
yangsyu@mail.ntue.edu.tw
[2] Institute of Information Science, Academia Sinica, Taipei City, Taiwan (R.O.C.)
cmwang@iis.sinica.edu.tw

Abstract. In research, automatic service composition (ASC) has been a widely studied academic subject for many years. However, this field still contains topics and issues that remain unidentified or uninvestigated. In this paper, we focus on one such unsolved problem of the ASC, elaborating on a current effort and future plan.

This recognized problem is caused by the difference between the formation of service descriptions used by human composers and that used by ASC approaches. In practice, engineers are used to write various development-related documents in natural language, such as their requirement specifications and software component descriptions. However, an exhaustive survey found that most existing ASC studies are assumed to take their required service descriptions in a tuple-based format. Although this difference and problem in theory can be sufficiently addressed using manual processing techniques (e.g., human transformation or extraction), we consider such human intervention to be inefficient, costly, and, most importantly, harmful to the level of automation of ASC. Thus, this study develops an automated solution to this problem.

We first introduce some necessary background knowledge and foundation so that the targeted problem can be fully understood and motivated. Then, the specific problem to be studied is clearly defined and exemplified along with a detailed explanation. Finally, the three key components to explore and address this research problem (dataset, approach, and evaluation) are discussed in detail, including the current work of the authors and proposals for future research.

Keywords: automatic service composition · service description · natural language processing · rule-based extraction · conditional random field · deep learning

1 Introduction

In academia, automated (Web) service composition (ASC/AWSC) has been a hotly and widely studied research subject for many years, and there are already plenty of ASC approaches and related tools, theories, and (reference) standards that have been

© The Author(s), under exclusive license to Springer Nature Switzerland AG 2023
Y. Zhang and L.-J. Zhang (Eds.): ICWS 2023, LNCS 14209, pp. 18–31, 2023.
https://doi.org/10.1007/978-3-031-44836-2_2

published and are available. However, there remain issues and topics that have never been identified or studied in ASC research. To improve the applicability and successful implementation of ASC, these unsolved problems must be clearly defined, thoroughly investigated, and properly addressed. This paper first identifies one such ASC issue – the tuple-based service descriptions used and assumed in most existing ASC studies – and then discusses its remedy. Because the proposed and targeted issue is in ASC, to ensure clear understanding, we introduce service composition (SC) and its automation (i.e., ASC/AWSC) in the remainder of this section. Then, the problem of interest is formulated and explained in detail in the next section.

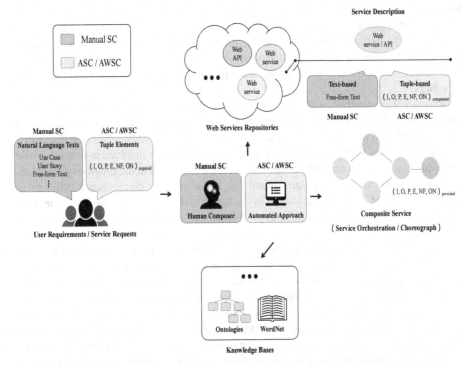

Fig. 1. Graphical process and comparison of design-time manual SC and ASC/AWSC.

Overall, the lifecycle of an SC can be divided into two stages: the design-time phase and runtime execution. A more complex model could exist, but for simplicity, in this study we introduce SC based on this basic model. More specifically, the discussion and introduction below exclusively focus on the first stage of SC, which concentrates on the entire and complete generation of a composite service (CS) from scratch to meet a received user request or customer requirement and, according to the proposed investigation, is also the primary concern and target of most surveyed ASC studies. As shown in Fig. 1, on its left-hand side, the creation of a CS (i.e., its design-time composition process) begins with a software requirement (service request), which is identical to most development process models proposed and used in software engineering [1]. Typically, such a requirement or request would be expressed using at least one of the formations widely used and developed in software requirement engineering, such as free-form texts, use case descriptions defined in UML, and user stories proposed in agile methods. The commonality between these different forms of demand expression is that they all consist of natural language statements to describe their writers' intentions: *natural language is used prevalently for expressing systems and software requirements* [2]. After having this stimulative information about what is required, a human composer, who is represented at the center of Fig. 1, takes time to read and analyze the message; assess and consider the available component services; and finally select and integrate a set of appropriate component services to design and produce a service orchestration or choreograph, which forms the desired CS, as shown on the right-hand side of Fig. 1. Regarding component services, the composer must understand and comprehend their specifications because programmers must carefully read the documents of their used program APIs before loading and calling them (e.g. functionality and nonfunctional properties) by inspecting their text-based service descriptions (on top of Fig. 1) because these available component services are often developed, offered, and owned externally by others.

Instead of manually composing services, researchers work on its automation, ASC, which is also shown in Fig. 1. Although ASC is a broad research field that includes and is associated with many different topics and aspects in detail, such as service discovery, matchmaking, and QoS prediction, overall, the basic elements involved in this automatic procedure resemble its manual version that we have explained in the previous paragraph. However, compared with regular/manual SC, some of these elements are different in their forms in ASC research, as shown in the figure and explained below. First, the most significant difference is that an ASC is performed automatically rather than by a human service composer, as shown at the center of Fig. 1. Second, the service descriptions involved in this automated process, which are the primary inspiration of this paper and this study work, including both the information of an intended/required service (i.e., a service requirement or composition request on the left-hand side of Fig. 1) and the descriptions for the available component services (on the top), are in forms of tuples, not in any of those natural language sentence-based formations introduced previously for software requirement engineering. In addition, the outcome and result of an instance of ASC (i.e., a CS) could be presented in a tuple-based way as well. Finally, for semantic ASC/AWSC, which has been widely considered a more sophisticated and advanced manner of automatic aggregation of services, at least one knowledge base, such as a self-defined domain ontology or a general WordNet, is required to have a reference or source of common/domain knowledge, as shown at the bottom of Fig. 1. As an exemplification, the above three types of service (description) correspond to the tuple-based required, component, and provided service types defined and used in an ASC study [3]. This process identified important differences between the formation of the service descriptions of ASC and the one used in the software development practice motivates this study.

Certainly, this problem, the processing (e.g., transformation or extraction) of natural language texts into their corresponding tuple-based elements, which is defined and explained in detail in Sect. 2, can be solved and addressed by human labor. However, this manual solution is inefficient and even ineffective. First, the biggest shortcoming of the involvement and intervention of humans is that it markedly decreases ASC's extent of automation and removes the goal and appeal of ASC, which is to reduce (or even entirely eliminate), as much as possible, manual tasks. Second, manually performing the handling process defined in Sect. 2 for the problem is both costly and time-consuming (and even impractical) because, as a set of materials/resources for composition, there could be numerous component services. For example, on ProgrammableWeb, over 15,000 WSs and Web APIs are registered and available. Similarly, the many incoming human-written, natural language sentence-based service requests and software requirements poses the same dilemma. Thus, a human labor-free solution for the problem is required to reach and have a fully automated composition of services. To our knowledge, this problem has never been identified, considered, or studied before; therefore, in Sect. 3, we elaborate on the authors' current effort and future research plan.

2 Problem

This section explains the identified and targeted problem in detail. One of the major findings of the proposed previous survey [4] of the service description approaches in ASC indicates the extensive adoption of a tuple-based formation for different types of service descriptions in this field of research. As reviewed and listed in [4], the set of tuple elements assumed and considered in an ASC study depends on its concern and coverage (awareness), and after a thorough investigation of existing ASC papers, as a universal service description model for ASC research, a generic, tuple-based paradigm proposed and used in the survey is:

$$<I, O, P, E, NF, ON>$$

where I, O, P, E, and NF are a described service's input, output, precondition, effect (postcondition), and nonfunctional property sets, respectively; and *ON connects to a knowledge ontology (or base) that formally and semantically defines the elements contained in other tuples* [4] (i.e., the component at the bottom of Fig. 1). Overall, as mentioned, which tuple elements are considered and used in an ASC study is determined by relevant aspects, and because different ASC considerations and their combinations have been studied in the past, a number of disparate groupings of these tuple elements have been used, such as $<I, O, P, E>$, $<I, O, QoS>$ and $<I, O, P, E, QoS>$, as comprehensively described in Table 1 of [4]. Due to limited space, we now provide an explanation with an assumption, where the most basic functional service description model is considered and used: $<I \text{ and } O>$.

As an example taken from an ASC study, a request that is acceptable to existing ASC approaches would be in the following format:

$I = $ (*Book title, Book author, Credit card information, Address that the book will be shipped to*),

$O = $ (*Payment from a credit card for the purchase, Shipping dates, Customs cost for the specific item*)

However, as explained in the Introduction, human demanders are used and preferable to, as below, express their intention as text in natural language:

"The user wishes to provide as inputs a book title and author, credit card information and the address that the book will be shipped to. The outputs of the desired composite service are a payment from the credit card for the purchase, as well as shipping dates and customs cost for the specific item."

Similarly, also sampled from an ASC research paper, the natural language sentence, which is *PatientByIDService takes as input a patient ID to return the patient's description*, describes the function of a component service. However, as mentioned before, to be usable in and compatible with most current ASC approaches, a tuple-based version of this service description, such as $I = (Patient\ ID)$ and $O = (Patient's\ description)$, is required.

More specifically and formally, this study's goal is to seek an effective and accurate automation (F) that takes a received natural language text-based service/software description (X) as its input and working foundation and then produces a set of corresponding tuple elements (Y) of the description as its processing result for subsequent ASC operations:

$$F : X \rightarrow Y$$

3 Solution

To solve this research problem, we consider three major issues that must be properly addressed: a dataset of ample natural language sentence-based service descriptions and their corresponding tuple-based labels; an automated process that can perform the task defined in the previous section or, in a more advanced and handy way, a technique or approach that is capable of finding such an automation automatically; and a quantitative standard for performance assessment for the developed automations upon an established dataset. Below, we discuss each of these issues in detail in dedicated sections, including this study's plan and current ongoing effort.

3.1 Dataset

First, before being able to develop an approach and measure its performance, an essential foundation is a collection comprising a sufficient number of problem instances and their corresponding labeling (i.e., answers). In this case, the instances and labels are natural language service descriptions and their tuple-based elements, respectively. Because we are the first to identify and investigate this research problem, to our knowledge, an available and valid dataset matching this study's goal does not exist before us; thus, we must build one. Regarding its construction, there are several considerations for the effectiveness, usability, and representativeness of such a dataset, including its scale, diversity, type of description, and labeling.

The first two concerns, each of which can also be viewed and used as a (quantitative) criterion of dataset, are critical to the development of an automation for the defined problem. As discussed in the next section, if such an automation is manually created, which we consider is a relatively primitive and inefficient way of solving the problem, then a small- or middle-scale dataset with at most hundreds of instances may be sufficient and more appropriate because manually observing and inducting from more cases probably would overload human developers. Thus, diversity, such as the variation of the structures and phrasing of natural language sentences, would be more critical and important for an automation's generality rather than quantity. However, if a meta-automation is used for the generation of automations, such as a machine learning-based technique or method, then it is likely that both the scale and diversity of the dataset matter. For example, due to the enormous number of neurons (weight values) comprised in their neural networks, deep learning (DL) techniques usually require tens of thousands, even millions, training cases (learning samples) to work. Overall, for both approach development and performance evaluation, we consider these two properties of the dataset as the higher the better.

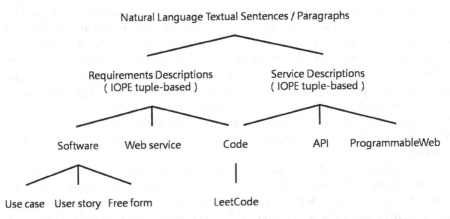

Fig. 2. Alternative sources of the planned under-construction service description dataset.

As mentioned in the Introduction, ASC involves three types of service descriptions. However, only two of them likely must be processed for ASC approaches and are therefore studied with this research problem. Also, we consider the descriptions of service/composition requests (requirements) and component services because these two types of information are indispensable when an ASC approach works to compose services. For the gathering and collection of such service descriptions, existing ASC papers and their illustrating composition examples can be a source, including both their demonstrated composition requests and component service specifications. However, insufficient quantities have been found to be a problem [5] (i.e., a threat to both diversity and, primarily, scale) because most ASC studies only present a few (typically only one) illustrations of composition upon a small set of component services. Thus, certainly, valid alternatives must be sought and used. Specifically, considering the two concerned properties, for service demands (i.e., composition requests), we plan to use existing software requirement datasets as an additional supplement because they are similar in essence (service/composition requests are also a type of software requirement). Regarding software requirements, a review of the literature and this study's data collection showed that such datasets can be written down and expressed in different formations in software engineering, including use case scenarios in UML, user stories in agile methods, and free-form texts (i.e., texts with specific restrictions/templates) [2], as introduced in Sect. 1. For both dataset diversity and approach generality, we consider that requirements in these paradigms (and the others that are also commonly used in software engineering practice but not mentioned in this study) should all be considered, included, and addressed properly, as has been done in some previous studies for the automated extraction and generation of graphical software (e.g., domain [2]) models from various forms of (i.e., unrestricted) natural language software requirements. When using a developed approach, no assumptions about the syntax and structure of its processable descriptions must be made. Finally, we discuss one more provider (alternative) of service demands in the next paragraph, *Leetcode*, which has been seen and used in a study as a massive collection of intended software functionalities. Conversely, regarding the descriptions of component services, current service repositories (e.g., *ProgrammableWeb*) and the textual explanations of their registered services are a straightforward and ample origin of this type of information. In addition, we consider that program API documents may be another abundant source for the proposed dataset construction because, as human-written descriptions of component services, these documents are also natural language declarations of (program) components in nature. The entire idea and big picture of the proposed planned under-construction service description dataset are shown in Fig. 2. Eventually, with a dataset built in this manner with the above roots, we believe that an adequate scale, diversity, and types of service descriptions for future research can be reached.

In a preliminary study [5], an extraction of the *Leetcode* problem set consisting of approximately 160 functionality statements and 10 composition requests from the ASC literature are used for both approach development and performance evaluation. However, apparently, this aggregation is deficient in all the aspects discussed previously (i.e., diversity, scale, and type). Thus, as a remedy and enhancement, the establishment of a complete service description dataset obeying prior ideas is ongoing. While the tagging of the input and output elements (IO tuples) for the functionality demands contained in the aggregation has been manually performed, we consider that two disparate perspectives regarding data labeling are worth discussing in more detail, including the detailedness of data labeling and untagged data. First, in the above data aggregation, the tokens (words and symbols) of sentences are marked in binary, and thus, a token is either an extraction target (i.e., part of an intended input/output element) or not. As an example, *this/0 service/0 generates/0 the/1 location/1 of/1 customer/1 (or this service generates (the location of customer)$_{TargetOutput}$)*, for which the result of extraction should be like $O = (the\ location\ of\ customer)$. However, this method lacks specifics and distinctions, which we consider might be a disadvantage or even an obstacle, particularly when using machine learning-based solutions, such as those using conditional random fields (CRFs), which we discuss and explain in the next section, because they provide users with insufficient details and poor variation. For example, for CRF, this leads to fewer distinguishable and definable features that likely would deteriorate the extraction result and performance. To investigate and solve the proposed problem more completely, more detailed and advanced remarking of problem instances could be helpful and useful, such

as *this service generates (((the location)$_{CoreOutput}$ (of customer)$_{AdjectivePhrase}$)$_{EntireOutput}$.*
However, this process certainly increases the cost of dataset establishment and tagging
that we discuss below for the second perspective. As anticipated, manual labeling of
a dataset is time-consuming, tedious, and error-prone, particularly when its scale is
large, as is required in the proposed study. However, unfortunately, carefully reviewing
and tagging data is necessary when referred to as answers and supervised learning.
To solve this issue, cutting-edge machine/deep learning technologies, such as pretrained
models, which required training with large untagged data; and fine-tuning, which adjusts
a pretrained model with a small amount of mission-specific labeled data, may be worth
trying and investigating for this study and application.

3.2 Approach

Regarding the resolution of this research problem, because it is basically a case and
application of natural language processing (NLP) involving information extraction (e.g.,
IO tuple elements) from human-written (service) descriptions, no matter what specific
(paradigm of) solution is used, a reliable NLP tool is indispensable for parsing and
providing essential linguistic knowledge for a subsequent solution (either an automation
or meta-automation) to perform as expected. Thus far, *Stanford CoreNLP* [6] has been
widely recognized as the best performing of such NLP tools. Therefore, this study uses
this tool as the foundation and provider of linguistic information for the proposed planned
and developed approaches, as shown at the top of Fig. 3.

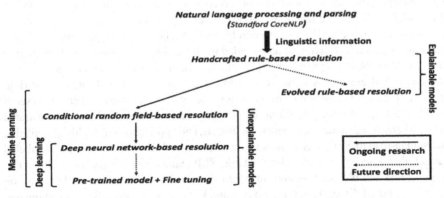

Fig. 3. Proposed research plan with an increasing level of automation.

The remainder of Fig. 3 shows a path that visualizes the proposed study plan. As
explained, the proposed ultimate goal aims to eliminate, as much as possible, human
intervention in the creation of a method or model for the problem defined in Sect. 2
so that a true automation (truly automated solution) with a minimized manual effort
can be obtained. However, such a goal is quite challenging and not instantly reachable
due to the complexity and difficulty of the targeted problem. Thus, when developing
the proposed method, we plan to explore the proposed problem step by step along a

route of increasing level of automation to have an insightful understanding and comprehensive solving (studying) of the problem, as shown in Fig. 3 and as described in detail below. The proposed research plan can be discussed and viewed as having several disparate dimensions, which are the method of production (manual, semiautomatic, and automatic), form (representation, such as *if-then-else*-based rules or neural networks), and understandability (explanability and/or interpretability) of a generated model.

For this targeted problem, [5] is the proposed first published research work, which can be characterized as, in terms of the three considered dimensions, a manually developed, NLP extraction rule-based, and human-understandable-model approach. In this research, as an initial study, the most straightforward and basic (primitive) paradigm for the resolution and addressing of such NLP applications has been used to preliminarily investigate this problem. More specifically, after an iterative and exhaustive human observation and analysis of the dataset established in [5], a set of NLP extraction rules were manually and incrementally developed and verified by the authors of [5]. Based on the experimental results of this preliminary study, the accuracy and performance of transforming functionality descriptions into their corresponding tuple-based elements is acceptable. However, the biggest weakness (also the deficiency of this type of solution) of this process is that the observation, analysis, enactment, and implementation of these NLP extraction rules is both time-consuming and labor-demanding, which we consider can and should be improved due to its inefficiency and heavy cost. To address this issue and research direction, we decide to take advantage of machine learning techniques, as shown in the two branches of Fig. 3.

Before diving into the left branch of Fig. 3, we first discuss the figure's smaller right branch. Considering the third concerned dimension (i.e., the understandability of a model), although the machine learning-based approaches on the left branch could significantly decrease (CRF) or even entirely eliminate (DL technology) human labor and intervention in the production of an intended model, unlike handcrafted NLP extraction rules, such as those proposed in [5], common machine learning models are hard to understand and explain by humans. To address this concern, as indicated in the right branch of Fig. 3, it is possible to automatically (genetically) evolve and generate a set of NLP processing rules for a problem or application, as has been tried and demonstrated in [7], where the advantages, benefits, usefulness, and applications of highly explainable and human-readable rule-based models can be found and seen. Thus, with a well-labeled dataset, theoretically human-understandable NLP extraction rules for the problem can be generated and obtained without manual effort, which we consider the best case on the two proposed dimensions (i.e., the first and last ones) and, thus, is worth trying and investigating (i.e., one of the proposed future research directions).

Conversely, along the left branch of Fig. 3, with a rising extent of automation, a planned track of solutions is shown and includes three separate stages/approaches. However, instead of the conditional random field (CRF), which appeared first on the branch, after [5], we first used the neural network models of DL to address the problem due to its powerful capability and many successful applications reported. Following the order of the left branch, we consider CRF to have a lower level of automation compared with DL because it requires its users to intervene to design and define a set of suitable feature functions before learning and running. However, with the small dataset built and used in [5], the evaluation of the generated neural network models discloses that they are nearly perfect in training performance (nearly 100 percent accurate) but poor in testing with unseen cases, which suggests that overfitting has occurred. We believe that this overfitting phenomenon is probably caused by the two contrary circumstances, the large number of variables (i.e., the weight values of neurons, usually hundreds of thousands of them at least) contained in a deep neural network model and the small dataset consisting of fewer than 200 problem instances for learning and fitting (i.e., an underdetermined system). Thus, before a large-scale dataset described in Section III A is available for the development and investigation of a DL-based solution, we decide to take one step back in terms of the level of automation and study the application of CRF to the proposed problem, as described in the next paragraph.

As with most techniques and models, CRF has advantages and disadvantages. Compared with DL networks, one of the advantages of CRF is that depending on the designed and used feature functions (the number of considered feature instances), its number of (weight) parameters that must be fitted and adjusted with training materials is typically much lower. Thus, in theory, unlike DL techniques and models that frequently require at least tens of thousands of instances and their tags to work due to their enormous neurons, CRF takes fewer cases to learn and fit, which matches the proposed current research circumstance and limitation that only a small dataset is available. However, this advantage of CRF also comes with a cost of poorer automation because for each specific problem, a set of appropriate feature functions must be manually identified and formulated in advance. Thus far, the ongoing and unpublished research of the authors that uses CRF can reach the same level of extraction performance as [5]. However, in [5], we spend dozens, even a few hundreds, of hours on developing its NLP extraction rules and approach, while by contrast, it takes a shorter time to identify a set of valid feature functions of CRF. More specifically, compared to the handcrafted rules-based approach in [5], CRF performs better in both the efficiency of approach development and the extent of automation, but one of its disadvantages is that even with much fewer model parameters, a CRF model is still not easy to explain and understand by humans. Overall, we consider that the model understandability of CRF is worse than that of handcrafted rules and better than that of DL networks. Regarding the level of automation, however, CRF is higher than handcrafted rules and lower than deep learning networks. Finally, regarding CRF, we are still working on the identification and formulation of its more efficient and important feature functions for the proposed application problem so that better performance and further insight can be obtained.

As shown in Fig. 3, the proposed next stage of approach development goes into deep learning. As discussed before, we have already tried and applied a DL neural network to address the proposed problem, although this preliminary trial presents a problematic result that suggests that more effort and deeper investigation must be performed. Regarding its technical details, in this initial study of DL for the proposed problem, we use the long short-term memory (LSTM) model, which is a type of recurrent neural network (RNN) in DL, because it can process both single data points and entire sequences of data (e.g., the dependencies across the disparate points of a data sequence), which is an important property that is naturally and intensively required in the proposed application and research because human sentences and descriptions, in essence, are sequences of words and phrases (units) that, except for the individual units, their entire context and the relationships between them must also be considered and handled as a whole. In addition, LSTM has also been successfully applied in many other NLP tasks and sequence labeling/learning applications, which is another reason for its adoption. Regarding the improvement and correction of this current failure of LSTM on the problem, as mentioned before, we consider that this result is probably caused by an overfitting LSTM model, for which three different solutions and potential directions have been planned or studied: (1) a larger dataset offering a greater number of training/learning cases, as discussed in Sect. 3. A; (2) decreasing the complexity of the model or adopting a model with a lower complexity (e.g., the proposed employment and trial with CRF); and (3) reducing the noise among data (i.e., denoising). Concerning the third point, because the currently available dataset comprises merely a small number of problem instances for learning and training, any type of noise likely causes severe overfitting and negatively affects the proposed approach and the resulting DL models. Thus, the identification and handling of the noises within the dataset would probably be necessary. For example, the replacement of a set of semantically or functionally equivalent words and phrases with a general term during the preprocessing stage could be helpful in avoiding overfitting.

Last, as an advanced study of the application of DL to solve the proposed problem, due to its recent popularity and success in various NLP tasks and applications [8], we plan to take advantage of pretrained models and their fine-tuning. More specifically, instead of training and fitting a DL model from scratch for a specific mission, such as what we have done before with LSTM, pretrained large-scale NLP neural models, such as BERT and GPT, could be used for the proposed problem. In this case, if applicable and useful, we no longer must work to generate a mission/task-specific DL model from scratch, which is both costly and time-consuming. Also, the gathering and labeling of a large-scale dataset for the proposed problem, which is also expensive and typically requires long computation times, such as that described in Sect. 3.1, likely would become unnecessary and avoidable. Regarding the fine-tuning of a pretrained model for the proposed purpose and application, because this training (transferring) takes only a relatively smaller mission/task-specific dataset, the proposed current data collection established and used in [5] might be instantly and directly applicable and triable. Overall, we consider that this study and application will likely markedly benefit from these cutting-edge DL technologies, as analyzed above. Thus, as drawn in the last stage of the left branch of Fig. 3, they are worth trying and investigating.

3.3 Evaluation

For this research subject, the criteria of the proposed assessment incorporate both time and accuracy. Regarding time, two different stages must be considered and measured separately, how long it takes to automate the problem (e.g., developing a set of extraction rules or fitting a CRF/DL model) and to generate a set of adequate tuple elements using a specific automation (a set of developed rules or a fitted CRF/DL model), respectively. At the first stage, the current observation is that the higher the level of automation is, the shorter the time taken to achieve automation. As mentioned previously, it takes a lot of time (e.g., dozens of hours) to observe and develop the rule-based approach presented in [5], while the training and generation of a CRF/DL model takes a much shorter duration.

Considering the pure model generation (training) time of ML, CRF is actually faster than LSTM (i.e., DL model) according to the proposed experiments because the former approach has fewer parameters (weight values) to adjust and fit. As explained before, however, CRF requires additional time for human involvement because it requires its human developers/users to manually identify and design a set of feature functions before running, which is typically time-consuming. Applying a pretrained model is expected to be more efficient in time because rather than creating a new DL model from scratch, only fine-tuning is required, which explains why a manner with superior automation is preferably wanted in this study. Regarding the second stage, we consider it unimportant because, regardless of which solution is used, it would not take too long to produce a result (i.e., much faster than the speed of human processing and extraction, at least), even with a DL model containing millions of neurons (or a pretrained model reaching a billion-level).

The second criterion, which is likely the primary concern of the performance evaluation of this research problem, measures both the correctness and completeness of the produced tuple elements with their corresponding ground truth data (i.e., labeled answers). Overall, this type of evaluation, which is common and regularly used in information retrieval and extraction, consists of two consecutive phases. First, a confusion/error matrix including four separate categories – true positive (TP), false-positive (FP), true negative (TN), and false-negative (FN) – must be counted and acquired. Then, based on the values of these four cases, we can easily calculate and obtain ultimate performance metrics (indicators), such as accuracy (TP + TN/TP + TN + FP + FN), precision (TP/TP + FP), recall (TP/TP + FN), and F1 score, as done in [5]. However, there is a potential problem found during the proposed evaluation. As an example, for a service description *with a customer ID, this service generates the public information of this customer, and the correct and complete element of the output tuple should be the public information of this customer.* However, in reality, different approaches may give different results with different levels of completeness (or correctness), such as *the information, the public information,* and *the information of this customer.* Without a common standard or consensus, different studies may treat and consider these incomplete outcomes differently (e.g., how to punish and count an incomplete element when making a confusion/error matrix and to what extent for each possible case), which would produce inconsistent scores, makes different studies incomparable with each other and is why we want to develop a utility providing, with the planned dataset, an impartial and handy performance evaluation for this research subject, as explained in detail below.

The last thing about the performance evaluation of this research topic is that as a public, large-scale dataset described in Sect. 3.1, a utility for making and facilitating a consistent, convenient, and quick performance assessment for researchers working on this problem is an important future goal. With the proposed planned dataset and this utility, the developers of different approaches can quickly and accurately calculate and understand the quantitative performance of their work, making precise and fair comparisons with others.

4 Conclusion

In this paper, we first introduce manual service composition and its automation, automatic service composition. Then, based on this introduction, we compare and describe the major differences between manual and automatic service composition, which may be a threat to automation due to the necessity of human intervention and processing, the formations of their used descriptions of services. After the targeted research issue has been defined and explained in detail, the proposed current achievement and future plan on the issues are presented exhaustively, including the dataset, approach, and evaluation of the issue.

During the proposed collection and observation of the current service descriptions and their alternatives, an important issue is identified: the desired targets, such as the input elements of a service, do not always explicitly appear in the text of its depiction; they can be considered and called implicit elements. More specifically, a software component (e.g., a Web API/service) can be explained and described from disparate perspectives, in different ways, and at unidentical levels of detail. For example, both the sentence *this hotel searching service takes a specific location as its input and generates a list of candidate hotels as output for its user* and the statement *this service provides a hotel searching functionality* could be describing the same service. However, the approaches introduced and planned in this paper can only process and obtain the targeted tuple elements from the former description and cannot address the second statement because the targets are not literally and explicitly contained in the statement. With sufficient domain knowledge and development experience, we believe that human engineers and developers can comprehend and manage both types of component/service descriptions adequately, manually determining what material is required (input) and what would be produced (output) with a service offering a hotel searching functionality. However, with the automations discussed in Section III B, it is impossible to extract and identify elements from a text that contains none of them. Such limitations and the inability to implicit elements, which can be processed, generated, and added by human engineers and developers with proper domain experience and knowledge, can be found in many past studies, such as [9], where only the concepts and their relationships that explicitly appear in the stated requirements will be extracted for the automatic construction and creation of a corresponding conceptual model. Because a large proportion of the surveyed and collected service descriptions and functionality statements are in this style (the majority of them, actually), we consider it a more challenging problem and advanced issue that must be deeply considered and properly addressed in the future for a better applicability and usefulness of the proposed solution.

Acknowledgment. This paper was partially sponsored by the Ministry of Science and Technology (Taiwan) under Grants Most111-2222-E-152-001-MY3 and Most110-2221-E-001-006-MY2.

References

1. Sommerville, I.: Software Engineering, 9/E. Addison-Wesley, Boston (2010)
2. Arora, C., Sabetzadeh, M., Briand, L., Zimmer, F.: Extracting domain models from natural-language requirements: approach and industrial evaluation. In: Presented at the Proceedings of the ACM/IEEE 19th International Conference on Model Driven Engineering Languages and Systems, Saint-Malo, France (2016). https://doi.org/10.1145/2976767.2976769
3. FanJiang, Y.-Y., Syu, Y.: Semantic-based automatic service composition with functional and non-functional requirements in design time: a genetic algorithm approach. Inf. Softw. Technol. **56**(3), 352–373 (2014). https://doi.org/10.1016/j.infsof.2013.12.001
4. Fanjiang, Y.-Y., Syu, Y., Ma, S.-P., Kuo, J.-Y.: An overview and classification of service description approaches in automated service composition research. IEEE Trans. Serv. Comput. **10**(2), 176–189 (2017)
5. Syu, Y., Tsao, Y.-J., Wang, C.-M.: Rule-based extraction of tuple-based service demand from natural language-based software requirement for automated service composition. In: Katangur, A., Zhang, L.J. (eds.) SCC 2021. LNCS, vol. 12995, pp. 1–17. Springer, Cham (2021). https://doi.org/10.1007/978-3-030-96566-2_1
6. Manning, C.D., Surdeanu, M., Bauer, J., Finkel, J.R., Bethard, S., McClosky, D.: The Stanford CoreNLP natural language processing toolkit. In: Proceedings of 52nd Annual Meeting of the Association for Computational Linguistics: System Demonstrations, pp. 55–60 (2014)
7. Shahrzad, H., Hodjat, B., Miikkulainen, R.: Evolving explainable rule sets. Presented at the Proceedings of the Genetic and Evolutionary Computation Conference Companion, Boston, Massachusetts (2022). https://doi.org/10.1145/3520304.3534023
8. Han, X., et al.: Pre-trained models: past, present and future. AI Open **2**, 225–250 (2021). https://doi.org/10.1016/j.aiopen.2021.08.002
9. Vidya Sagar, V.B.R., Abirami, S.: Conceptual modeling of natural language functional requirements. J. Syst. Softw. **88**, 25–41 (2014). https://doi.org/10.1016/j.jss.2013.08.036

SPaMeR: Securing Patient Medical Records in the Cloud - A Microservice and Brokerless Architecture Approach

T. B. Nam[1]($\boxtimes$), H. G. Khiem[1], M. N. Triet[1], K. V. Hong[1], T. D. Khoa[1],
Q. T. Bao[1], N. T. Phuc[1], M. D. Hieu[1], V. C. P. Loc[1], T. L. Quy[1], N. T. Anh[1],
Q. N. Hien[1], L. K. Bang[1], D. P. N. Trong[1], N. T. K. Ngan[2], H. Son[3],
and H. H. Luong[1]($\boxtimes$)

[1] FPT University, Can Tho city, Vietnam
namtbce161036@fpt.edu.vn, huonghoangluong@gmail.com
[2] FPT Polytechnic, Can Tho city, Vietnam
[3] RMIT University, Ho Chi Minh city, Vietnam

Abstract. The expansion of Internet of Things (IoT) technologies has revolutionized various sectors, one of the most critical being healthcare. The effective management of Patient Medical Records (PMRs) is an area where IoT plays a significant role, and its integration with Cloud Computing offers an enormous opportunity to enhance data accessibility, efficiency, and cost-effectiveness. However, the challenge of securing PMRs in the cloud remains a key concern. This paper introduces SPaMeR, an innovative IoT platform based on microservice and brokerless architecture, tailored to address this challenge and the specific requirements of healthcare environments. SPaMeR platform incorporates and extends the core functionalities of the IoT platform designed in our previous work - data collection, device and user management, and remote device control - while specifically addressing six critical issues for healthcare data: a) secure and reliable transmission of medical data, b) energy efficiency for healthcare devices, c) high-speed and accurate data collection from medical devices, d) robust security mechanisms to protect sensitive patient information, e) scalability to accommodate the ever-growing number of patients and medical devices, and f) compliance with healthcare data regulations and standards. To demonstrate the effectiveness and feasibility of SPaMeR, we provide a comprehensive evaluation with two distinct healthcare scenarios. Our results indicate significant improvements in the areas of data security, energy efficiency, and system scalability compared to traditional healthcare platforms.

Keywords: Medical record · Internet of Things · microservice ·
gRPC · Single Sign-On · brokerless · Kafka · micro-service · RBAC

1 Introduction

The Internet of Things (IoT) has been steadily proliferating across various sectors including smart cities, healthcare, supply chains, industry, and agriculture.

By 2025, an estimated 75.44 billion IoT devices are projected to be interconnected [3]. Specifically, IoT has revolutionized many sectors, and healthcare stands as a significant beneficiary. The transformative potential of IoT in healthcare extends to patient care, data collection, and healthcare management, shaping a new era of medical practice [26]. As the linchpin of IoT applications, the IoT platform is pivotal in coordinating data collection, managing devices and users, and enabling remote device control.

Recently, there has been an intensified focus on the optimal design of these platforms, particularly in critical sectors such as healthcare. In these sectors, the availability and accuracy of data can substantially influence patient outcomes. Nonetheless, conventional medical IoT systems often prioritize big data or participant access control aspects, thereby downplaying the importance of accurate, rapid, and efficient data collection, power redundancy, and system expansion [26].

To address this, various architectural models have been proposed, including the 5-layer architecture: Things, Connect, Collect, Learn, and Do, introduced by [5]. This model clarifies distinct roles within an IoT Platform, mapping them to different layers for efficient implementation. While the applicability of IoT spans diverse areas, finding a universally fitting architecture remains challenging. Regardless, three features are universally indispensable for an IoT system: i) data collection; ii) device and user management; and iii) remote device control. These features align with the Things, Connect, and Collect layers in the proposed model [5]. Each layer, however, presents unique challenges that can impede the efficiency and security of the IoT system. Things, the physical devices that collect data or perform actions, often grapple with power, processing, and bandwidth limitations [15]. The Connect layer, comprising various IoT protocols like HTTP, CoAP, XMPP, AMQP, and MQTT, must sync with the hardware and network processing capabilities of Things. Despite the pros and cons of each [3,30], MQTT is frequently preferred for constrained network communications owing to its superior transmission speed and energy efficiency [14]. However, MQTT has known security limitations, with threats to Integrity, Availability, and Authentication and Authorization mechanisms [2,19].

The Collect layer is a software ensemble that accumulates data from Things via the Connect layer. The architecture of this layer is determined by the protocol used in the Connect layer. This paper scrutinizes a Collect layer architecture that uses MQTT, a popular protocol in IoT frameworks employed by prominent companies such as IBM, Amazon, and Microsoft [9]. MQTT's dependence on a pub/sub architecture and a centralized broker, however, could lead to single point failures [20], with no guarantees for message storage or the order of delivery [13]. Given the sensitive nature of medical data, robust security mechanisms and stringent privacy protections are vital to thwart unauthorized access and malicious exploits [25].

To surmount these challenges, this paper introduces SPaMeR, a groundbreaking platform that utilizes a brokerless architecture at the Collect layer and a microservice architecture. The platform employs the gRPC protocol to directly collect medical data from IoT devices (e.g., wearable/smart devices, sensors), thereby eliminating the need for a central broker to coordinate topic-based messages. The amassed medical data is then relayed for storage, distribution, and further processing. Coupled with a microservice architecture, SPaMeR guarantees system robustness, scalability, availability, and load-bearing [1]. Additionally, SPaMeR integrates an RBAC (role-based access control) and hierarchical user management model (tree structure) to enhance authorization, thus bolstering the security of users, devices, and communication channels. Through this framework, SPaMeR aims to secure patient medical records in cloud environments, thereby strengthening the security and reliability of healthcare IoT systems. SPaMeR not only tackles conventional healthcare IoT platform challenges but also introduces advanced features like real-time alerts for medical teams and optimized access control for patient records [25].

The remainder of this paper is organized as follows. Related work is discussed in Sect. 2. SPaMeR platform and the corresponding proof-of-concept are described in Sects. 3 and 4, respectively. Sections 5 and 6 present the test results and the discussion & future work. The paper's conclusion with a summary in Sect. 7.

2   Related Work

In this section, we discuss prior research on brokerless architectures in IoT, IoT platforms based on microservices, and OAuth for IoT. These three categories form the foundation of our proposed SPaMeR architecture. Each of these domains has been studied independently in previous works, and our study aims to unite these areas into a singular, cohesive system, strengthening the security of patient medical records in the cloud.

2.1   Brokerless Architecture in IoT

Alif Akbar Pranata et al. [21] built a water quality monitoring system following a brokerless pub/sub architecture. However, their work does not discuss system scalability and security measures. Similarly, Battery Lv et al. [20] proposed a brokerless IoT system to mitigate common security issues and single-point failure problems. Their approach was well-suited for banking systems but may be limited in scenarios requiring high-speed data transmission. Ryo Kawaguchi et al. [16] explored the potential of a distributed MQTT broker-based system to avoid single-point failures. Yet, the necessity of operating numerous physical servers and sharing user location information pose cost and privacy challenges.

2.2   IoT Platform Based on Microservice

The concept of microservices in IoT has been explored by several researchers. Sergio Trilles et al. [29] built a functional microservice architecture for IoT applicable to Smart Farming, still dependent on a broker architecture for data collection. Luca Bixio et al. [4] extended the Senseioty platform with a streaming data model for real-time data collection. However, their architecture lacks comprehensive security measures and device control mechanisms.

2.3   OAuth and the Internet of Things

In their work, Paul Fremantle et al. [8] successfully demonstrated the feasibility of using OAuth, a commonly utilized open standard for access delegation, within the Internet of Things (IoT) context. Specifically, their implementation focused on enabling access control via the MQTT (Message Queuing Telemetry Transport) protocol, a lightweight messaging protocol designed for constrained devices and high-latency networks, frequently used in IoT applications.

The paper's experimental results convincingly proved that an IoT client could utilize the OAuth token to authenticate with an MQTT broker effectively. This important finding posits OAuth not merely as a suitable authorization mechanism for traditional web applications but also as a practical choice for low-capability hardware devices found in the IoT space. To achieve this, the researchers implemented the Web Authorization Protocol to generate access tokens, which were then integrated into the MQTT client. This demonstrated a powerful synergy between the OAuth standard and the MQTT protocol, expanding the horizons of possible applications in the IoT sphere. Moreover, the paper outlines the detailed procedure of a combined OAuth and MQTT implementation, particularly focusing on the internal communication process between the MQTT broker and the MQTT client.

However, an area of concern in their implementation is the reliance on RESTful services over the HTTP/1.1 protocol for packet transfer. This approach can potentially be inefficient in the IoT context, given that it might consume a substantial amount of bandwidth and energy - a limitation discussed earlier in the Introduction section. To address this, our work aims to incorporate OAuth with Single Sign-On (SSO) into a service specifically designed for device authentication. The goal is to leverage the security benefits of OAuth and the user convenience provided by SSO in an IoT setting. Importantly, we propose the usage of gRPC (Google's high-performance, open-source universal RPC framework) for device communication with this service, given its efficiency and benefits over traditional HTTP/1.1. This approach is geared towards optimizing bandwidth usage and energy consumption, thus mitigating the limitations of the implementation discussed in Fremantle et al.'s work.

3   SPaMeR Architecture

The SPaMeR architecture adopts a microservice design to foster improved scalability and robustness. This approach involves breaking down the architecture into small, loosely coupled services, which can independently develop, deploy, and scale. Each service is designed to fulfill a specific function and can communicate with others to complete more complex tasks. This architecture is divided into three core layers: the Device layer, the Server layer, and the Patient layer (Fig. 1).

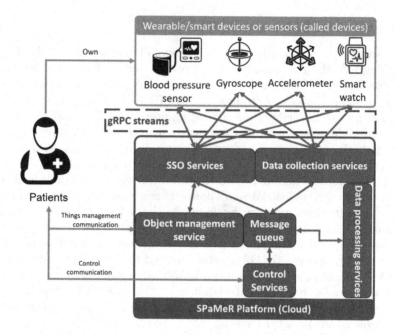

Fig. 1. SPaMeR Platform as Microservice Architecture

Device Layer. The Device layer is the frontline of the architecture, encompassing physical IoT devices such as smartwatches, blood pressure monitors, gyroscopes, accelerometers, and other devices capable of gathering medical data from patients. Each of these devices features an embedded system, which collects patient medical data and transmits it to the Server layer via the gRPC protocol, an efficient, high-performance framework for inter-service communication.

In addition to data transmission, this layer is also responsible for device control. Devices receive control commands either from the Patient layer or from the medical data processing service within the Server layer. These commands adjust the behavior of devices based on the data they collect, thus providing a dynamic, responsive system.

Server Layer. At the heart of the architecture is the Server layer. This layer consists of several microservices, each designed to perform specific tasks, demonstrating the advantages of the microservice architecture in managing complexity by breaking down system functions into manageable, independent services. These microservices include:

– **Data Collection Service:** This service interfaces with the Device layer, collecting medical data from authenticated devices. It also conveys control commands from the Patient layer or medical data processing service to the devices.

- **Single Sign-On (SSO) Service:** Authentication of devices and patients is handled by this service, which follows the OAuth protocol to provide secure, token-based authentication.
- **Object Management Service:** This service is responsible for managing system objects such as patients and devices, ensuring accurate tracking and control over these elements.
- **Control Service:** This service provides an interface for patients to remotely control their devices, forwarding the commands to the Device layer.
- **Medical Data Processing Service:** This service performs the critical task of analyzing collected medical data. It also stores system logs and issues control commands to devices based on predefined triggers.
- **Message Queue:** As the messaging backbone of the Server layer, the Message Queue handles inter-service communication, transporting messages between different services.

Patient Layer. The Patient layer forms the user-facing part of the architecture. Patients interact with the system via the Internet of Devices service. Authentication by the SSO service is required for patients to access and interact with the services in the Server layer. This secure access control mechanism helps maintain patient privacy and data security.

4   Implementation

To better comprehend the SPaMeR platform's design, it's vital to elaborate on the components in the system and their interactions. This section provides a detailed description of the software architecture and the communication workflows that underpin the system's operation.

4.1   Patients

Patients are the end-users of the IoT services offered by our platform. To accommodate various user scenarios, a hierarchical patient model is established. This model is akin to a tree structure, with parent patients being able to create and manage their child patients. This setup offers flexibility and scalability, especially useful for large-scale deployments involving multiple levels of patients, such as in a healthcare institution.

Each patient has a unique patient_id value conforming to the UUID standard, managed by the Object Management Service. This unique identifier allows for efficient and error-free patient data management. Patients use their patient_id and password to request an access token from the Single Sign On service, which is subsequently used to authorize their interactions with the system.

4.2   Devices

Devices represent the various physical devices or applications owned by the patients. These could range from wearable health monitors to home-based healthcare equipment. To register a device, the patient owning the device must provide a valid OAuth token. Once the device is registered, the patient embeds the access token into their devices. Only devices bearing a valid access token can communicate with the Medical Data Collection Service. This token-based authentication mechanism enhances security by ensuring that only legitimate devices can transmit data to the Server layer, thereby protecting the system from potential data breaches or denial-of-service attacks.

4.3   Communication Workflow

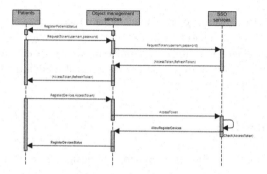

Fig. 2. The patients and their devices initialization processes

Initialization Workflow. The system initialization begins with the registration of a patient. Once registered, the patient requests an access token using their patient name (i.e., account) and password. The system returns an access token and refresh token as per the OAuth standard. With the access token, the patient can then register their devices with the system, enabling the creation of device information in the Object Management Service (Fig. 2).

Medical Data Collection Workflow. Data collection commences with devices sending their access tokens to the SSO Service for authentication. Once authenticated, the devices are permitted to stream medical data to the Medical Data Collection Service. This service then funnels the collected data to the Message Queue. As a robust inter-service communication mechanism, the Message Queue provides other services, such as the Data Processing Service, access to the medical data stream. This multi-step process ensures that data collection is secure, efficient, and capable of handling large volumes of data from numerous devices (Fig. 3).

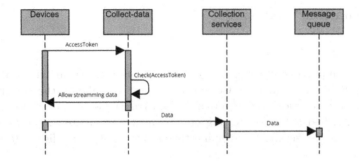

Fig. 3. Medical data collection process

Control Workflow. The control workflow allows patients to remotely control their devices. Patients initiate this process by sending their access token and the desired command to the Control Service. The SSO Service validates the access token. If the token is valid, the Control Service forwards the command to the Message Queue. The Message Queue, in turn, delivers the command to the Medical Data Collection Service, which finally transmits the command to the targeted devices. This cascading workflow ensures that device control commands are securely and efficiently transmitted, allowing for real-time device control.

The SPaMeR platform utilizes a robust and scalable microservice architecture to securely manage patient medical records in the cloud. This system design allows for secure data collection, processing, and remote device control, ensuring that patient health data can be accurately and securely managed. It forms an integral part of the wider Internet of Medical Things ecosystem, allowing for continuous health monitoring and informed medical decisions, thereby significantly enhancing healthcare outcomes (Fig. 4).

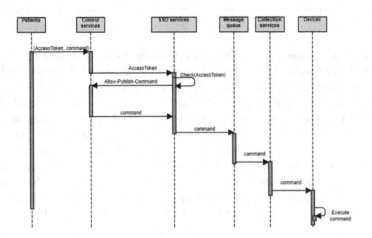

Fig. 4. Control Workflow in the SPaMeR System

5   Evaluation Scenarios

5.1   Environment Setup

The evaluation process of our proposed SPaMeR platform began with the implementation of the Medical Data Collection service. To validate the performance of our platform, particularly in terms of data transmission speed and scalability, we established a specific testing environment and created multiple scripts to emulate real-life scenarios involving the transmission of medical data over a cloud server.

Two core scenarios were formulated to evaluate the efficacy of a broker-less architecture employing the gRPC protocol versus a brokered architecture using the MQTT protocol. Both of these protocols are well-known for their efficiency and reliability in IoT communications. However, their performance characteristics differ under different circumstances, making this evaluation integral to optimizing our platform. The source codes for these scenarios can be found in our Github repository in the previous version of this paper [27], namely the Medical Data Collection service[1] and the MQTT streaming[2]. A visual representation of these scenarios is provided in Fig. 5.

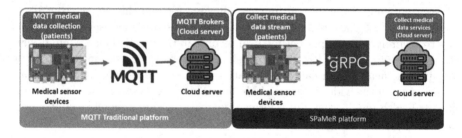

Fig. 5. Comparison scenarios of communication speed between gRPC and MQTT

The test environment comprised two testbeds, each incorporating a medical sensor devices (Raspberry Pi) module and an Amazon EC2 Server configured similarly to mirror the common resources of a typical IoT cloud server environment. This configuration enabled a fair and accurate comparison of the two protocols. Conversely, the first testbed used medical sensor devices and cloud server to deploy an MQTT client and broker, leveraging the MQTT protocol for packet transmission. In the second testbed, the and implemented the Medical Data Collection service, relying on the gRPC protocol for data transmission. This setup represented our platform's broker-less architecture, where communication is direct and efficient, albeit requiring more processing power. This setup highlighted the benefits and drawbacks of a brokered architecture where

---

[1] https://github.com/thanhlam2110/iot-platform-collect-data-service.
[2] https://github.com/thanhlam2110/mqtt-streaming.

an intermediary manages communication, providing better scalability but potentially limiting data transmission speed. These environmental settings provided the basis for a comprehensive evaluation of our SPaMeR platform's performance and ability to efficiently manage and transmit medical data in a cloud server setup.

5.2 Message Delivery Speed Test Case

One of the critical factors when considering the transmission of medical records in a cloud environment is the speed of message delivery. The reason for emphasizing this aspect is twofold. Firstly, healthcare applications often require real-time or near-real-time data transmission to provide accurate and timely diagnoses or recommendations. Secondly, medical emergencies demand immediate data access, and any delay in data delivery could have severe consequences.

Given this background, our first test case is designed to evaluate the message delivery speed, specifically focusing on comparing the performances of the gRPC and MQTT protocols. We perform this comparison across three runs, and the results are presented in Table 1. In particular, the performance comparison between gRPC and MQTT under different Quality of Service (QoS) settings, i.e., QoS-0 and QoS-2, was the first test case in our evaluation process. It is significant to understand that MQTT provides three levels of QoS, including:

- **QoS-0 (At most once):** The message is sent only once and not acknowledged, making it the fastest but least reliable level.
- **QoS-1 (At least once):** The message is retransmitted until it is acknowledged, providing assurance of message delivery but no guarantee of duplication.
- **QoS-2 (Exactly once):** The message is assured to be delivered exactly once by using a four-step handshake process, offering the highest level of message assurance but also being the slowest.

Table 1. Performance comparison between two scenarios (i.e., gRPC vs MQTT (QoS-0; QoS-2)) in terms of delivery speed (in seconds).

Sending time	gRPC	MQTT (QoS-0)	MQTT (QoS-2)
1st	54 s	269 s	can't complete test
2nd	50 s	294 s	can't complete test
3rd	52 s	295 s	can't complete test
Average	52 s	286 s	can't complete test

From Table 1, we can see that the gRPC protocol significantly outperforms MQTT in terms of message delivery speed. On average, gRPC took just 52 s to complete the transmission, whereas MQTT (Quality of Service level 0) took around 286 s. Interestingly, MQTT (Quality of Service level 2) was unable to complete the test, suggesting potential issues with handling the large amount of medical data in this scenario.

The results highlight the advantage of gRPC in the case of transmitting patient medical records, reinforcing our decision to utilize this protocol within the SPaMeR platform for efficient and rapid data transmission. The platform's ability to swiftly deliver medical data could prove instrumental in time-sensitive healthcare scenarios, contributing to more efficient medical responses and potentially improving patient outcomes.

5.3   Disrupted Connection Test Cases

The resilience of a platform when handling disruptions in the connection, especially when dealing with sensitive data such as medical records, is of utmost importance. As such, we conducted a series of tests to assess the impact of connection disruptions between data publishers and subscribers in our proposed SPaMeR platform. The test model is depicted in Fig. 6. These tests compared the number of received messages in scenarios both with and without the implementation of the SPaMeR platform when a disrupted connection occurred. In the scenario without the SPaMeR platform, the subscriber could only receive a single message - the most recent message sent by the publisher when the disruption occurred. This outcome is tied to the 'retain' functionality of the MQTT protocol, which, when activated, allows the MQTT broker to store only the most recent message published by the publisher. This message is then received by the subscriber once it reestablishes its connection to the MQTT broker[3]. In stark contrast, while utilizing the SPaMeR platform, the subscriber could receive all the messages published by the publisher, even in the event of a disrupted connection. This capability is attributed to the Kafka message queue embedded within the platform, ensuring data consistency and mitigating data loss. This result

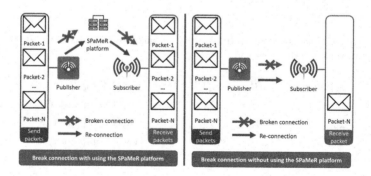

Fig. 6. The simulation of broken connection issue in the received messages when system in the two approaches

---

[3] http://docs.oasis-open.org/mqtt/mqtt/v3.1.1/os/mqtt-v3.1.1-os.html.

not only illustrates the robustness of the SPaMeR platform when handling connection disruptions but also underscores its suitability for transmitting sensitive patient medical records reliably, even in challenging network conditions.

6   Discussion

6.1   Our Observation

Our work sought to present an improved method for ensuring the secure and reliable transmission of patient medical records within an IoT context. Based on the results of our evaluations, several key discussion points have emerged.

Firstly, the brokerless architecture combined with the gRPC protocol, as implemented in the SPaMeR platform, offers a significant performance advantage in terms of message delivery speed over the MQTT protocol, traditionally used in IoT systems. This was particularly noticeable in our Message Delivery Speed Test Case, where the gRPC implementation demonstrated a markedly faster average delivery speed. This advantage can be crucial in real-world healthcare applications where timely access to data can directly impact patient care. Secondly, the evaluation demonstrated the resilience of our platform under disrupted connection scenarios. It is inevitable that connection disruptions will occur in real-world deployments due to various factors. In such scenarios, the ability of the SPaMeR platform to ensure data integrity and continuity, thanks to the Kafka message queue, sets it apart from traditional MQTT based approaches. This resilience and reliable data delivery become even more important when the data in question are sensitive patient medical records. Finally, the use of a microservice architecture lends a high degree of modularity and scalability to the platform. This structure allows the system to be easily expanded or modified, facilitating a more agile and adaptable approach to system design and development. The microservice architecture combined with the brokerless system and the use of gRPC protocol allows our platform to handle large-scale IoT deployments effectively and efficiently, making it suitable for enterprise-level healthcare IoT applications.

However, while the initial evaluations are promising, further testing and refinement will be necessary to ensure that the SPaMeR platform can meet the rigorous demands of real-world deployments fully. Key areas for future work could include detailed security assessments, comprehensive load testing, and in-depth analysis of platform performance under various network conditions. Additionally, assessing the platform's ability to handle various types of medical data and integrate with different IoT devices will be important for broad adoption in the healthcare industry. In summary, our work presents a significant step towards the reliable and secure management of patient medical records in the IoT domain. It paves the way for more advanced, efficient, and reliable healthcare IoT systems, thereby aiding the broader mission of improving healthcare delivery and outcomes.

6.2   Prospective Developments

Considering the need for scalability to accommodate an expanding number of devices and users demanding swift authorization, addressing security concerns such as object security, privacy, and availability remain central challenges for future investigation.

Concerning security, further research will aim to introduce our solutions in various real-life scenarios. Particular attention will be devoted to the healthcare domain, given its vital societal role and the sensitive nature of data involved [6, 7,24]. This could include applications such as patient health record management, telemedicine, and hospital information systems.

Regarding privacy, we are considering the application of attribute-based access control (ABAC) [12,23] to manage the authorization processes of the SPaMeR Platform. ABAC's capacity to use dynamic policies could provide enhanced flexibility in controlling access based on various factors, including the user's role, the requested resource, and the context of the request [22,28,31].

Lastly, to enhance system availability and robustness against single points of failure, we plan to investigate the benefits of incorporating blockchain technology into the platform's infrastructure [10,11,25]. By decentralizing data storage and management, blockchain could significantly increase the system's resilience and guarantee data integrity [17,18], making it an attractive solution for the future development of the SPaMeR Platform.

7   Conclusion

Our work proposed the SPaMeR platform's design and architecture, leveraging microservices and a brokerless approach, offering a robust and scalable solution for securing patient medical records in a cloud environment. By utilizing the gRPC protocol, we've presented a substantial enhancement in message delivery speed over traditional MQTT-based approaches, a critical factor in healthcare applications where real-time data accessibility can directly affect patient care. Additionally, the robustness of SPaMeR in handling connection disruptions ensures the integrity and continuity of data transmission, an indispensable requirement when dealing with sensitive patient medical records. The system's resilience stems from the implementation of the Kafka message queue, thereby ensuring no data loss occurs, a significant improvement over MQTT's handling of connection disruptions. The use of a microservice architecture enhances the scalability and modularity of the platform, enabling efficient and effective management of large-scale IoT deployments, positioning SPaMeR as a suitable choice for enterprise-level healthcare IoT applications.

Despite these promising results, we recognize the need for additional testing and refinement to fully prepare SPaMeR for the demanding real-world deployment conditions. Future work should focus on rigorous security assessments, comprehensive load testing, detailed analysis of performance under varying network conditions, and the capability to handle diverse medical data types and integrate with a wide range of IoT devices.

Acknowledgement. We would like to extend our deepest gratitude to Engineer Le Thanh Tuan and Mr. Lam Nguyen Tran Thanh for their invaluable contribution and insight throughout the conceptualization, execution, and assessment of this project.

References

1. Ali, M., Ali, S., Jilani, A.: Architecture for microservice based system. A report (2020)
2. Anthraper, J.J., Kotak, J.: Security, privacy and forensic concern of MQTT protocol. In: Proceedings of International Conference on Sustainable Computing in Science, Technology and Management (SUSCOM). Amity University Rajasthan, Jaipur (2019)
3. Bansal, M., et al.: Application layer protocols for internet of healthcare things (IoHT). In: 2020 Fourth International Conference on Inventive Systems and Control (ICISC), pp. 369–376. IEEE (2020)
4. Bixio, L., Delzanno, G., Rebora, S., Rulli, M.: A flexible IoT stream processing architecture based on microservices. Information **11**(12), 565 (2020)
5. Chou, T.: Precision-Principles, Practices and Solutions for the Internet of Things. McGraw-Hill Education, New York (2017)
6. Duong-Trung, N., et al.: On components of a patient-centered healthcare system using smart contract. In: Proceedings of the 2020 4th International Conference on Cryptography, Security and Privacy, pp. 31–35 (2020)
7. Duong-Trung, N., et al.: Smart care: integrating blockchain technology into the design of patient-centered healthcare systems. In: Proceedings of the 2020 4th International Conference on Cryptography, Security and Privacy, pp. 105–109 (2020)
8. Fremantle, P., Aziz, B., Kopecký, J., Scott, P.: Federated identity and access management for the internet of things. In: 2014 International Workshop on Secure Internet of Things, pp. 10–17. IEEE (2014)
9. Fuentes Carranza, J.C., Fong, P.W.: Brokering policies and execution monitors for IoT middleware. In: Proceedings of the 24th ACM Symposium on Access Control Models and Technologies, pp. 49–60 (2019)
10. Ha, X.S., Le, H.T., Metoui, N., Duong-Trung, N.: DeM-CoD: novel access-control-based cash on delivery mechanism for decentralized marketplace. In: 2020 IEEE 19th International Conference on Trust, Security and Privacy in Computing and Communications (TrustCom), pp. 71–78. IEEE (2020)
11. Ha, X.S., Le, T.H., Phan, T.T., Nguyen, H.H.D., Vo, H.K., Duong-Trung, N.: Scrutinizing trust and transparency in cash on delivery systems. In: Wang, G., Chen, B., Li, W., Di Pietro, R., Yan, X., Han, H. (eds.) SpaCCS 2020. LNCS, vol. 12382, pp. 214–227. Springer, Cham (2021). https://doi.org/10.1007/978-3-030-68851-6_15
12. Hoang, N.M., Son, H.X.: A dynamic solution for fine-grained policy conflict resolution. In: Proceedings of the 3rd International Conference on Cryptography, Security and Privacy, pp. 116–120 (2019)
13. Hwang, H.C., Park, J., Shon, J.G.: Design and implementation of a reliable message transmission system based on MQTT protocol in IoT. Wireless Pers. Commun. **91**(4), 1765–1777 (2016)
14. Jaikar, S.P., Iyer, K.R.: A survey of messaging protocols for IoT systems. Int. J. Adv. Manage. Technol. Eng. Sci. **8**(II), 510–514 (2018)

15. Karagiannis, V., Chatzimisios, P., Vazquez-Gallego, F., Alonso-Zarate, J.: A survey on application layer protocols for the internet of things. Trans. IoT Cloud Comput. **3**(1), 11–17 (2015)

16. Kawaguchi, R., Bandai, M.: Edge based mqtt broker architecture for geographical IoT applications. In: 2020 International Conference on Information Networking (ICOIN), pp. 232–235. IEEE (2020)

17. Le, H.T., et al.: Introducing multi shippers mechanism for decentralized cash on delivery system. Int. J. Adv. Comput. Sci. Appl. **10**(6) (2019)

18. Le, N.T.T., et al.: Assuring non-fraudulent transactions in cash on delivery by introducing double smart contracts. Int. J. Adv. Comput. Sci. Appl. **10**(5), 677–684 (2019)

19. Lee, S., Kim, H., Hong, D.K., Ju, H.: Correlation analysis of MQTT loss and delay according to QoS level. In: The International Conference on Information Networking 2013 (ICOIN), pp. 714–717. IEEE (2013)

20. Lv, P., Wang, L., Zhu, H., Deng, W., Gu, L.: An IoT-oriented privacy-preserving publish/subscribe model over blockchains. IEEE Access **7**, 41309–41314 (2019)

21. Pranata, A.A., et al.: Towards an IoT-based water quality monitoring system with brokerless pub/sub architecture. In: 2017 IEEE International Symposium on Local and Metropolitan Area Networks (LANMAN), pp. 1–6. IEEE (2017)

22. Son, H.X., Dang, T.K., Massacci, F.: REW-SMT: a new approach for rewriting XACML request with dynamic big data security policies. In: Wang, G., Atiquzzaman, M., Yan, Z., Choo, K.-K.R. (eds.) SpaCCS 2017. LNCS, vol. 10656, pp. 501–515. Springer, Cham (2017). https://doi.org/10.1007/978-3-319-72389-1_40

23. Son, H.X., Hoang, N.M.: A novel attribute-based access control system for fine-grained privacy protection. In: Proceedings of the 3rd International Conference on Cryptography, Security and Privacy, pp. 76–80 (2019)

24. Son, H.X., et al.: Towards a mechanism for protecting seller's interest of cash on delivery by using smart contract in hyperledger. Int. J. Adv. Comput. Sci. Appl. **10**(4) (2019)

25. Son, H.X., Nguyen, M.H., Vo, H.K., Nguyen, T.P.: Toward an privacy protection based on access control model in hybrid cloud for healthcare systems. In: Martínez Álvarez, F., Troncoso Lora, A., Sáez Muñoz, J.A., Quintián, H., Corchado, E. (eds.) CISIS/ICEUTE -2019. AISC, vol. 951, pp. 77–86. Springer, Cham (2020). https://doi.org/10.1007/978-3-030-20005-3_8

26. Thanh, L.N.T., et al.: IoHT-MBA: an internet of healthcare things (IoHT) platform based on microservice and brokerless architecture. Int. J. Adv. Comput. Sci. Appl. **12**(7) (2021)

27. Thanh, L.N.T., et al.: Sip-MBA: a secure IoT platform with brokerless and micro-service architecture. Int. J. Adv. Comput. Sci. Appl. **12**(7) (2021)

28. Thi, Q.N.T., Dang, T.K., Van, H.L., Son, H.X.: Using JSON to specify privacy preserving-enabled attribute-based access control policies. In: Wang, G., Atiquzzaman, M., Yan, Z., Choo, K.-K.R. (eds.) SpaCCS 2017. LNCS, vol. 10656, pp. 561–570. Springer, Cham (2017). https://doi.org/10.1007/978-3-319-72389-1_44

29. Trilles, S., González-Pérez, A., Huerta, J.: An IoT platform based on microservices and serverless paradigms for smart farming purposes. Sensors **20**(8), 2418 (2020)

30. Verma, S., Rastogi, M.A.: IoT application layer protocols: a survey. J. Xi'an Univ. Archit. Technol. VII **57** (2020)

31. Xuan, S.H., et al.: Rew-XAC: an approach to rewriting request for elastic ABAC enforcement with dynamic policies. In: 2016 International Conference on Advanced Computing and Applications (ACOMP), pp. 25–31. IEEE (2016)

Applying Blockchain Technology for Privacy Preservation in Android Platforms

H. G. Khiem[1]([⊠]), T. B. Nam[1], M. N. Triet[1], H. L. Huong[1], T. D. Khoa[1],
Q. T. Bao[1], N. T. Phuc[1], M. D. Hieu[1], V. C. P. Loc[1], T. L. Quy[1], N. T. Anh[1],
Q. N. Hien[1], L. K. Bang[1], D. P. N. Trong[1], N. T. K. Ngan[2], H. Son[3],
and K. V. Hong[1]([⊠])

[1] FPT University, Can Tho, Vietnam
khiemhgce160922@fpt.edu.vn, KhanhVH@fe.edu.vn
[2] FPT Polytechnic, Can Tho, Vietnam
[3] RMIT University, Ho Chi Minh City, Vietnam

Abstract. Android applications (called apps) are an integral part of our digital lives, with an ever-growing user base generating massive amounts of data every day. Despite privacy measures in place, such as the Android permission model, there persists a significant privacy concern due to factors like centralized data storage and lack of transparency. This paper presents a novel approach to enhance privacy preservation in Android platforms, focusing specifically on managing 'dangerous' permissions related to sensitive health data. We propose a hybrid architecture that combines traditional data processing for regular data with a blockchain-based system for handling sensitive data, thus offering enhanced security, transparency, and user control. Our detailed evaluation using Ethereum Virtual Machine (EVM) compatible platforms (i.e., BNB, Fantom, Celo, and Matic) shows the feasibility and effectiveness of our approach, with the Fantom platform proving the most suitable due to its low transaction cost and optimal gas limit. We acknowledge that the successful implementation of our proposed solution relies on stakeholder acceptance. Therefore, we outline strategies for convincing both service providers and Android OS producers to consider this transformative approach. This paper offers a pioneering view into using blockchain technology to address the persistent privacy concerns in the Android app ecosystem.

Keywords: Android apps · Data security · Privacy preservation · Permission · Blockchain · BNB · Fantom · Celo · Matic

1 Introduction

The omnipresence of Android apps in contemporary society is indisputable, with a vast array of utility programs that have embedded themselves into daily routines, from navigation tools like Google Maps, to social networking platforms

Y. Zhang and L.-J. Zhang (Eds.): ICWS 2023, LNCS 14209, pp. 47–61, 2023.
https://doi.org/10.1007/978-3-031-44836-2_4

like Facebook, and fitness trackers such as Fitbit. With over 2.6 million apps available on the Google Play store as of March 2023[1] (i.e., 2.67 million apps, after surpassing 1 million apps in July 2013), the Android system's prevalence continues to surge, fostering a globally interconnected network of users. According to App Annie's 2021 report, Android users spent over 3.5 trillion hours on apps[2]. For example, Facebook has 2.94 billion monthly active users, it also has 1.96 billion users that are visiting the social networking site on a daily basis[3].

However, alongside this digital revolution, an escalating concern about privacy has emerged. The Pew Research Center reported in 2019 that around 81% of the public feels they have little or no control over the data collected about them by both companies and the government[4]. Moreover, a survey conducted by NortonLifeLock in 2019 revealed that 72% of consumers are worried about their privacy when using mobile apps, with concerns varying from identity theft to unauthorized access to personal information[5].

Android adopts a permission model for managing access to sensitive data and performing certain actions[6]. apps must request permissions from users, and users can grant or deny these permissions either during installation or runtime. Additionally, app stores like Google Play Store implement review processes and policies to ensure app compliance with privacy guidelines. This allows users to review app permissions, ratings, and user feedback to make informed decisions about privacy risks (e.g., Tiktok's privacy policy[7]). Data safety policies provide additional safeguards, requiring developers to be transparent about their data practices and ensure data protection[8]. To address this problem, we summarize several approaches which detailed in Sect. 2.

Traditional methods to protect user privacy in Android apps face several challenges. Centralized data storage, a common feature, can lead to a "single point of failure" that significantly increases the risk of data breaches and unauthorized access [4]. These methods often lack transparency, making it difficult for users to understand and control how their data is collected, processed, and shared. This lack of transparency impedes trust-building, possibly deterring users from using the service due to privacy concerns [1,13]. This also provide limited user control over personal data. Users often can't manage what data is collected, how it's used, or who it's shared with, which raises potential privacy concerns [14].

Blockchain technology, a decentralized and immutable ledger, provides enhanced security and data integrity [11]. Its transaction transparency and security make it an effective tool for various apps, including privacy preservation in Android systems. However, it is not a silver bullet solution that can replace exist-

---

[1] http://bit.ly/3Nduhcg.

[2] https://technologymagazine.com/digital-transformation/app-annie-38-trillion-hours-spent-mobiles-2021.

[3] https://bit.ly/3CzGfbo.

[4] http://pewrsr.ch/3PjVOLW.

[5] https://bit.ly/447dheI.

[6] https://developer.android.com/guide/topics/permissions/overview?hl=en.

[7] https://www.tiktok.com/legal/page/row/privacy-policy/en.

[8] https://bit.ly/467Mkct.

ing data processing strategies. The current methods, optimized for performance and usability, are vital for app functionality. Therefore, we propose a hybrid approach that combines the efficiency of traditional data processing with the robust security of blockchain technology.

Our strategy retains traditional processing for 'normal' data, ensuring the preservation of app functionality and data processing effectiveness. Conversely, for sensitive or 'dangerous' data (i.e., Protection level: dangerous), which can potentially infringe on user privacy, we integrate a blockchain-based system. This system handles sensitive data with enhanced security, transparency, and user control. All data access or transactions are transparent and auditable, fostering user trust. In our proof-of-concept, we focus on managing 'dangerous' permissions (i.e., BODY_SENSORS; BODY_SENSORS_BACKGROUND specifically related to the motion/health/medical data (called medical data), given its sensitive nature and the high value placed on privacy in healthcare contexts. We aim to demonstrate how our proposed approach can provide a balanced, secure, and effective method for managing data in Android apps, with a particular emphasis on preserving user privacy (see Sect. 4 for more detail).

2   Related Work

In our paper, we propose a novel approach that is currently not widely adopted in the field. As such, there is a lack of comparable state-of-the-art methodologies that utilize blockchain technology for privacy preservation in Android platforms. However, it is important to consider other prevalent approaches addressing the broader topic of privacy preservation in Android platforms. These primarily fall into two most common ones: malware analysis and sensitive data encryption.

2.1   Malware Analysis

Malware analysis focuses on identifying and mitigating malicious software that may compromise user privacy. This includes techniques such as static and dynamic analysis, machine learning-based detection, and behavior analysis.

For example, Talha et al. [18] developed APK Auditor, a system for detecting malicious apps based on permission analysis. It comprised Android clients, a signature database, and a central server. APK Auditor used static analysis to capture permission requests and calculate malicious scores. In the same approach, Jianmao et al. [19] introduced MPDroid, an approach for evaluating target app risk based on minimum permissions. It used collaborative filtering and clustering techniques. Moreover, Enck et al. [7] proposed TaintDroid, an Android platform extension that tracked privacy-sensitive data flow in third-party apps. It labeled apps as privacy violations when personal data was transmitted to a third party. Another study by Moutaz et al. [2] considered a set of dangerous permissions identified by Google[9].

---

[9] https://developer.android.com/reference/android/Manifest.permission.

However, a limitation of these approaches is that they provide binary detection (malicious/benign), which may not be practical in assisting users with their decision-making. To address this, Son et al. [14,16] proposed a new approach which focused on the risk estimation based on the app's data collection and sharing behavior. Then, they process the app recommendation system [15] to suggest the most suitable app for individual based on their privacy preferences.

While the aforementioned studies have made significant contributions to the field of privacy preservation in Android platforms, they also present several limitations. For instance, APK Auditor [18] and MPDroid [19] rely heavily on permission analysis and static analysis, which may not be sufficient to capture all potential privacy risks. Even the risk estimation approach proposed by Son et al. [14,16] and their subsequent app recommendation system [15] do not fully address the need for a robust, transparent, and user-controlled platform for managing sensitive data.

In contrast, our paper addresses these limitations by integrating a blockchain-based system into Android platforms. This system handles sensitive data with enhanced security, transparency, and user control, providing a balanced, secure, and effective method for managing data in Android apps. All data access or transactions are transparent and auditable, fostering user trust. Furthermore, our approach retains traditional processing for 'normal' data, ensuring the preservation of app functionality and data processing effectiveness. We believe that our proposed approach represents a significant contribution to the ongoing effort to preserve user privacy on Android platforms.

2.2 Sensitive Data Encryption

Sensitive data encryption is a prevalent approach in privacy preservation in Android platforms. This method involves encoding user data in a way that only authorized parties can access it. Several studies have explored this approach, each with its unique contributions.

Chen et al. [5] proposed AUSERA, an automated tool for detecting security vulnerabilities in Android apps. Zhang et al. [20] discussed the vulnerability of Android external storage and proposed solutions to prevent sensitive information disclosure. Fan et al. [8] proposed HPDROID, an automated system that identifies GDPR compliance violations in mobile health applications. Mia et al. [12] conducted a comparative study on HIPAA technical safeguards assessment of Android mHealth applications. Haupert et al. [10] assessed the state of Android app hardening and proposed two attacks against a leading Runtime Application Self-Protection (RASP) product. Chen et al. [6] and Sengupta et al. [13] proposed blockchain-based systems for preserving medical data privacy. Balasubramanium et al. [3] conducted a survey on data privacy and preservation using blockchain in healthcare organizations.

While these studies have made significant contributions to the field, they also have several limitations. Most notably, they rely heavily on the developers' security knowledge and diligence, and they do not provide a comprehensive solution for managing a wide range of sensitive data. Furthermore, some of these studies focus primarily on healthcare data and do not address the broader range of sensitive data handled by Android apps. Others do not propose a specific implementation for Android platforms. Our proposed blockchain-based system addresses these limitations by providing a robust, transparent, and user-controlled platform for managing sensitive data in Android apps. We believe that the integration of blockchain technology represents a promising frontier in the ongoing effort to preserve user privacy on Android platforms.

3 Background

3.1 Android OS and Permission System

Android is an open-source operating system used primarily for mobile devices, such as smartphones, tablets, or wearable devices. It is developed by Google and based on the Linux kernel. Android provides a rich application framework that allows developers to build innovative apps and games for mobile devices in a Java language environment.

One of the key aspects of Android is its permission system, which is designed to protect the privacy of users. When developers create an app, they need to specify in the app's manifest file what types of user data the app needs to access, such as the user's location, contacts, camera, microphone, etc. These are known as permissions. There are different levels of permissions, but we focus on the two most popularity one (i.e., Normal and Dangerous). The detail of each level is described below:

– **Normal permissions:** These cover areas where your app needs to access data or resources outside the app but where there's very little risk to the user's privacy or the operation of other apps. For example, the ability to set the time zone is a normal permission.
– **Dangerous permissions:** These cover areas where the app wants data or resources that involve the user's private information, or could potentially affect the user's stored data or the operation of other apps. For example, the ability to read the user's contacts is a dangerous permission.
– **Signature permissions:** These are permissions that the system grants only if the requesting app is signed by the same certificate as the app that declared the permission.
– **Special permissions:** These are permissions that have a different workflow for the user to grant the permission. For example, the "Draw over other apps" or "System alert window" permission is a special permission.

When an app is installed on an Android device, the system asks the user to grant the permissions that the app requests. For apps targeting Android 6.0 (API level 23) and higher, the user isn't notified of any app permissions at installation time. Instead, the app must request permissions as it needs them, and the system shows a dialog to the user asking for the permission. The Android permission protect user data and app integrity, but developers must use it responsibly and only request permissions that are necessary for their app to function.

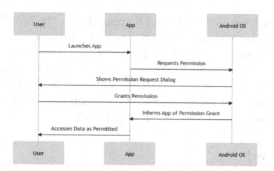

Fig. 1. The user data collection via the permission system in Android OS

Figure 1 presents a step-by-step diagram illustrating how an app collects user data via the permission system in Android OS. In the Android permission system, these three components interact to ensure that apps only have access to the data and device features that the user has explicitly granted. This system is designed to protect the user's privacy and security by giving them control over their own data.

– **User:** The user is the individual who interacts with the Android device and its applications. They have control over which permissions they grant to each app on their device. The user's role in the permission system is to consciously decide which permissions to grant based on their understanding of why an app might need such access.
– **App:** The app refers to any application installed on the user's Android device. Each app has a specific set of features and functionalities, some of which may require access to certain data or other features on the device. In the context of the permission system, the app's role is to request the necessary permissions from the Android operating system and then operate within the confines of those granted permissions.
– **Android OS:** Android OS, or Android Operating System, is the software that runs on the user's device. It manages all of the hardware and software resources on the device, including apps. In the context of the permission system, the Android OS acts as the intermediary between the app and the user. It receives permission requests from apps, presents these requests to the user in a standardized format, and then communicates the user's decision back to the app.

Moreover, Fig. 1 presents six step to collect the user data via the permission system. Firstly, he process begins when the user opens the app on their Android device. This could be an app that the user has just installed or an app that they have been using. If the app needs to access certain data or features on the device that require permissions (such as location data, camera, contacts, etc.), it then sends a request to the Android operating system. This request specifies the permissions that the app needs. Upon receiving the request from the app, after that, the Android operating system generates a dialog box. This dialog box is displayed to the user and it clearly states the permissions that the app is requesting. Next, the user has the option to either grant or deny the permissions. If the user grants the permissions, the Android operating system records this choice and will not ask the user for these permissions again for this app unless the app is reinstalled or the data is cleared. Once the user has granted the permissions, the Android operating system, then, informs the app. This is done through a callback method in the app's code, letting the app know that it now has the necessary permissions. Finally, the app can now access the user's data or device features as permitted with the necessary permissions granted. It's important to note that the app can only access the data or features that were specified in the granted permissions. For example, if the app was granted permission to access the user's location, it can now retrieve this data. This process ensures that apps cannot access sensitive data or features without the user's explicit permission, providing a level of security and privacy for the user.

3.2 Blockchain

A blockchain is composed of a series of blocks, each containing a list of transactions. Each block includes a cryptographic hash of the previous block, a timestamp, and transaction data. This design makes a blockchain resistant to modification of its data because once recorded, the data in any given block cannot be altered retroactively without alteration of all subsequent blocks, which requires consensus of the network majority.

One of the key features of blockchain technology is its decentralized nature. Unlike traditional centralized databases, where a single entity has control over all the data, a blockchain distributes the data across many different nodes in a peer-to-peer network. Each node in the network has a copy of the entire blockchain, and all nodes work together to validate new transactions and record them on the blockchain. This decentralization enhances the security of the system, as it removes single points of failure and makes it extremely difficult for any malicious actor to alter the data on the blockchain. Another important feature of blockchain technology is its transparency and auditability. Every transaction on the blockchain is visible to all participants in the network, and every transaction is permanently recorded on the blockchain, creating an immutable audit trail. This transparency helps foster trust among participants, as it ensures that no transaction can be altered or deleted once it has been recorded on the blockchain. Blockchain technology also enables the use of smart contracts, which are self-executing contracts with the terms of the agreement directly written into code. Smart contracts automatically execute transactions when predefined conditions are met, eliminating the need for a trusted third party. This feature can be used to automate a wide range of processes and applications, from financial transactions to supply chain management.

Due to the limitation of scope, in this paper, we just show a basic definition of the blockchain technology. For more detail, we suggest the reader refer [21] as a formal definition as well as the opportunities and challenges.

4   Approach

Figure 2 presents the idea of integrating blockchain technology with the permission process in Android systems to enhance privacy preservation. The architecture can be described in the following steps:

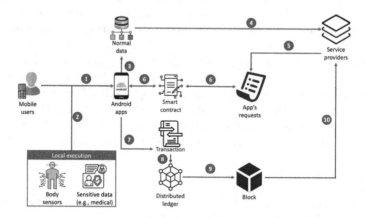

Fig. 2. Our proposed model architecture

A user first opts to install an application - in this context, a medical application. We emphasize on medical applications due to the highly sensitive nature of health-related data. Even small pieces of medical data can lead to potential privacy breaches as they could potentially identify individuals. When the app requests access to data via the dangerous permissions to collect the medical data, the app potentially gains access to a user's detailed or aggregated data (second step). In our system, such requests entail an extended process, from step 5, which involves outlining the data requirements, to step 10, which entails sending responses to the service providers. In the third step, if the app requests normal data, it follows the normal permissions procedure as outlined in Sect. 3. The app can gather these types of data without any added security measures. If the service provider requests the transmission of the collected normal data to its servers (i.e., globle execution), this fourth step comes into play. Our approach ensures the secure transmission of these data to the service provider's servers. Otherwise, the fifth step, if an app requests sensitive data through dangerous permissions (e.g., we consider the two ones BODY_SENSORS; BODY_SENSORS_BACKGROUND to collect the medical data), it is required to detail its request. The request must include information on the purpose of usage, the type of data required, and the possibility of third-party usage. This process is justified because of (i) the availability of most of this information in the app's privacy policy, and (ii) requirements set by data privacy regulations, like GDPR[10], which necessitates apps to demonstrate secure data handling processes. The user, on their device, next validates

---

[10] https://gdpr-info.eu/.

the request through a smart contract in the sixth step. This allows the user to have an active role in the decision-making process concerning their data. The use of smart contracts enhances transparency and places control in the hands of the user. Once validated, the user's decision is logged as a transaction between them and the service providers (step 7). This is reminiscent of the traditional permission system. However, with the introduction of machine learning techniques, future decisions can refer to the initial decisions, reducing the need for constant user intervention [17]. All these transactions are securely stored in a distributed ledger (step 8). The user has three response options: i) non-consent, which means denying data collection, ii) full consent, which grants full access to the service providers' requests without any changes, iii) partial consent, where the user allows the service providers to collect abstracted, aggregated data or a subset of the requested data. The ninth step is then encrypted using the service provider's public key with elliptic curve cryptography [9]. This ensures that only the intended service provider can decrypt and access the response. We use Non-Fungible Token (NFT) technology to encapsulate the responses, ensuring each response is unique and non-interchangeable. Finally, the block, represented as an NFT, is transferred to the service provider. This final step completes the interaction, providing the service provider with the necessary (and permitted) data, and leaving a traceable, immutable record of the transaction on the blockchain.

This architecture offers several advantages over the traditional permission system in Android platforms. With the integration of blockchain, the system achieves greater transparency and auditability since every transaction is recorded and verifiable. The use of smart contracts ensures user control and consent, enabling the user to specify which data can be accessed. Also, by using NFTs and elliptic curve cryptography, data integrity is maintained, and secure data sharing is achieved. This innovative approach helps build trust between users and service providers and promotes collaboration while complying with data privacy regulations. Furthermore, the scalability and efficiency of blockchain make this approach a sustainable choice for future privacy-preserving systems.

5   Experiments

Our study aims to propose a blockchain-based platform that acts as a distributed ledger, primarily focusing on steps 8 and 9 as depicted in Fig. 2. This is the preliminary phase of our broader research goal.

5.1   Methodology

In developing our platform, we considered blockchain platforms that support the Ethereum Virtual Machine (EVM), including Binance Smart Chain (BNB Smart Chain)[11]; Polygon[12]; Fantom[13]; and Celo[14]. These platforms were chosen over

---

[11] https://github.com/bnb-chain/whitepaper/blob/master/WHITEPAPER.md.
[12] https://polygon.technology/lightpaper-polygon.pdf.
[13] https://whitepaper.io/document/438/fantom-whitepaper.
[14] https://celo.org/papers/whitepaper.

open-source alternatives such as those within the Hyperledger ecosystem (e.g., Hyperledger Fabric) due to their compatibility with EVM and broad acceptance in the decentralized application (DApp) development community. As a part of this research, we implemented our approach on four different blockchain platforms that support the Ethereum Virtual Machine (EVM) – BNB, MATIC, FTM, and CELO. One of the key contributions of this article is the collection and analysis of transaction fees associated with these platforms, using their respective testnet coins. We have made these implementations publicly accessible, serving as a contribution to the broader community[15]. The implementations on each platform can be found at the corresponding platforms, such as BNB[16], MATIC[17], FTM[18], CELO[19].

Fig. 3. The transaction info (e.g., BNB Smart Chain)

For the chosen EVM-supported platforms, we analyzed the transaction fee and the gas limit. The transaction fee is a crucial metric since it directly impacts the operational costs of running DApps on the blockchain. It is charged to process a transaction and varies depending on the complexity of the transaction and network congestion. The gas limit, on the other hand, refers to the maximum amount of gas the user is willing to spend on a transaction. It ensures the user's protection from spending more than they intend due to errors in the smart contract. We evaluated three common functions on these platforms:

1. Creating the user's response - This function is essential as it manifests the user's consent level (i.e., not allowing data collection, allowing partial or full collection of medical data) - see Sect. 4 for more details.
2. Creating a Non-Fungible Token (NFT) - The user response is encrypted using the service provider's public key and encapsulated into an NFT. This ensures the integrity and confidentiality of the user response.

---

[15] Our implementation models were released on 11/24/2022, 8:44:53 AM UTC.
[16] https://testnet.bscscan.com/address/0xafa3888d1dfbfe957b1cd68c36ede4991e104a53.
[17] https://mumbai.polygonscan.com/address/0xd9ee80d850ef3c4978dd0b099a45a559fd7c5ef4.
[18] https://testnet.ftmscan.com/address/0x4a2573478c67a894e32d806c8dd23ee8e26f7847.
[19] https://explorer.celo.org/alfajores/address/0x4a2573478C67a894E32D806c8Dd23EE8E26f7847/transactions.

3. Transferring the NFT - The NFT is then transferred to the service provider, providing an immutable record of the user's response.

Though encryption plays a significant role in our approach, it is not thoroughly discussed in this paper due to its broad scope. Detailed encryption methodologies and their analysis will be provided in subsequent versions of this work[20]. Figure 3 illustrates one of our evaluations - a successful installation on the BNB Smart Chain. Similar procedures and evaluations were conducted on the other three platforms. We designed and implemented smart contracts in Solidity to evaluate their execution cost across these platforms in their respective testnet environments. This approach aimed to determine the most cost-efficient platform for our system deployment. We further delve into the details, focusing on the cost implications of performing contract creation, generating Non-Fungible Tokens (NFTs) (as shown in Fig. 4), and updating NFT ownership address, which is essentially retrieving and transferring the NFTs (see Fig. 5).

Fig. 4. NFT creation   **Fig. 5.** NFT transfer

5.2 Transaction Fee

In our study, we compared the transaction fees incurred for the operations of Contract Creation, NFT Creation, and NFT Transfer across four different blockchain platforms - BNB Smart Chain, Fantom, Polygon (MATIC), and Celo. The detailed results of this comparison are presented in Table 1. On the BNB Smart Chain, the transaction fees are 0.0273134 BNB ($8.43) for contract creation, 0.00109162 BNB ($0.34) for creating an NFT, and 0.00057003 BNB ($0.18) for transferring an NFT. The Fantom platform showcased lower transaction costs, with contract creation costing 0.00957754 FTM ($0.001849), NFT creation at 0.000405167 FTM ($0.000078), and NFT transfer

Table 1. Transaction fee

	Contract Creation	Create NFT	Transfer NFT
BNB Smart Chain	0.0273134 BNB ($8.43)	0.00109162 BNB ($0.34)	0.00057003 BNB ($0.18)
Fantom	0.00957754 FTM ($0.001849)	0.000405167 FTM ($0.000078)	0.0002380105 FTM ($0.000046)
Polygon	0.006840710032835408 MATIC ($0.01)	0.000289405001852192 MATIC ($0.00)	0.000170007501088048 MATIC ($0.00)
Celo	0.007097844 CELO ($0.004)	0.0002840812 CELO ($0.000)	0.0001554878 CELO ($0.000)

---

[20] The proof-of-concept of our proposed model is available in https://github.com/SonHaXuan/medical-record-Blockchain-NFT.

at 0.0002380105 FTM ($0.000046). The Polygon (MATIC) platform showed even lesser costs, with 0.006840710032835408 MATIC ($0.01) for contract creation, 0.000289405001852192 MATIC (almost negligible in USD terms) for NFT creation, and 0.000170007501088048 MATIC (also nearly negligible in USD terms) for NFT transfer. Lastly, Celo incurred fees of 0.007097844 CELO ($0.004) for contract creation, 0.0002840812 CELO (almost negligible in USD terms) for creating an NFT, and 0.0001554878 CELO (also nearly negligible in USD terms) for transferring an NFT. From this comparison, it is evident that the transaction fees vary considerably across the four platforms, which can have significant implications for the selection of the most cost-effective platform for deploying our approach.

5.3   Gas Limit

Apart from transaction fees, another crucial aspect to consider while deploying smart contracts on a blockchain platform is the gas limit. In Ethereum-based platforms, the gas limit pertains to the maximum amount of gas that a user is willing to spend on a transaction. A higher gas limit means that the transaction can perform more operations. Our study evaluates this attribute across the four platforms under consideration - BNB Smart Chain, Fantom, Polygon (MATIC), and Celo. The findings are summarized in Table 2.

Table 2. Gas limit

	Contract Creation	Create NFT	Transfer NFT
BNB Smart Chain	2,731,340	109,162	72,003
Fantom	2,736,440	115,762	72,803
Polygon	2,736,284	115,762	72,803
Celo	3,548,922	142,040	85,673

In the BNB Smart Chain, the gas limits for contract creation, NFT creation, and NFT transfer are 2,731,340, 109,162, and 72,003, respectively. On the Fantom platform, the corresponding gas limits are slightly higher at 2,736,440 for contract creation, 115,762 for creating an NFT, and 72,803 for transferring an NFT. The Polygon (MATIC) platform exhibits similar gas limits with 2,736,284 for contract creation, 115,762 for NFT creation, and 72,803 for NFT transfer. Finally, on the Celo platform, the gas limits are the highest among the four platforms. The gas limits for contract creation, NFT creation, and NFT transfer on Celo are 3,548,922, 142,040, and 85,673 respectively. This analysis reveals that Celo has the highest gas limits, which might imply a higher computational complexity or a larger size of the contracts deployed on this platform compared to the others. It's crucial to consider these factors along with the transaction fees to select the most suitable and cost-efficient platform for our proposed approach.

6   Discussion

6.1   Our Finding

The results of our analysis, as shown in Tables 1 and 2, indicate that Fantom is the most suitable platform for our proposed system. While BNB Smart Chain and Celo demonstrated lower gas limits, their transaction fees were considerably higher. Polygon (MATIC), on the other hand, had the lowest transaction fees but similar gas limits as Fantom.

Fantom offers a beneficial balance of lower transaction fees and competitive gas limits. The transaction fees on the Fantom platform, as our analysis revealed, are significantly lower than BNB Smart Chain and Celo, making it a cost-effective choice. Moreover, its gas limits are comparable to or lower than the other platforms, implying that Fantom can efficiently handle our smart contracts' operations, which is critical to ensuring a smooth and effective execution of our proposed system. Another advantage of Fantom is its high throughput and fast confirmation times, which can improve the user experience and the overall performance of our system. This further strengthens our choice of Fantom as the most suitable platform for our proposed privacy-preserving Android system.

6.2   Remark

This study presents a comprehensive and practical approach for leveraging blockchain technology to secure sensitive user data, particularly in the context of health applications. The proposed architecture has the potential to significantly enhance privacy and data security within Android platforms, given that both service providers (e.g., app developers) and Android OS producers agree to its deployment. While the technical aspects of our proposal seem to be feasible and beneficial, it is crucial to acknowledge that the successful implementation of this approach relies heavily on stakeholder acceptance and cooperation. We propose a strategy to garner this acceptance, detailed below.

For Service Providers: App developers or service providers can enhance their users' trust by implementing robust data privacy protocols, which can, in turn, foster a more loyal and engaged user base. By deploying blockchain-based systems like ours, service providers can enable greater transparency, allowing users to have direct control over their data, and to trace and verify data transactions. This can distinguish them from competitors, thus increasing their market share and user trust. Moreover, the implementation of our approach could also contribute to ensuring compliance with data protection regulations, such as the GDPR, thereby reducing legal risks for service providers.

For Android OS Producers: Android OS producers can significantly enhance the security profile of their platforms by integrating blockchain technology into their existing permission systems, especially concerning "dangerous" permissions that manage access to sensitive data. The proposed model not only provides enhanced transparency but also empowers users with granular control over their data, which may boost user trust in the platform. By embedding the current dangerous permission system with our blockchain approach, Android OS producers can set a new standard in data privacy and security (called S&P data), positioning themselves as leaders in the global technology market.

In general, the successful implementation of our blockchain approach in Android platforms will likely require both a comprehensive understanding of its technical components and an effective strategy for securing stakeholder acceptance. As we continue to refine and develop our approach, we remain committed to fostering robust discussions about S&P data, and to exploring innovative ways to enhance these critical aspects of our increasingly digital world.

7   Conclusion

In this paper, we have presented a novel approach, applying blockchain technology for privacy preservation in android platforms, to enhance privacy and data security for Android applications, with a specific focus on medical apps. We introduced a detailed architecture that leverages blockchain technology to regulate access to sensitive user data, enforcing robust controls on permissions and ensuring transparency of data transactions. Our evaluation on four EVM-supported platforms (BNB, MATIC, FTM, CELO) showed the feasibility and effectiveness of our approach. Notably, the Fantom platform emerged as the most suitable option for our work, due to its low transaction costs and optimal gas limit settings. However, it's important to note that these results might differ with the fluctuation in the cryptocurrency market.

In our discussion, we acknowledged that the successful deployment of our approach heavily relies on stakeholder acceptance. Hence, we proposed strategies to persuade both service providers and Android OS producers. Future work will address the encryption measurement for further ensuring data privacy and reducing the potential risks. As technology continues to evolve, we believe that our work contributes significantly to the ongoing discourse about user privacy and data security on Android platforms, laying the groundwork for more transparent, secure, and user-friendly applications.

References

1. Al-Natour, S., et al.: An empirical investigation of the antecedents and consequences of privacy uncertainty in the context of mobile apps. Inf. Syst. Res. **31**(4), 1037–1063 (2020)
2. Alazab, M., et al.: Intelligent mobile malware detection using permission requests and API calls. Futur. Gener. Comput. Syst. **107**, 509–521 (2020)
3. Balasubramanium, S., et al.: A survey on data privacy and preservation using blockchain in healthcare organization. In: International Conference on Advance Computing and Innovative Technologies in Engineering, pp. 956–962. IEEE (2021)

4. Bandara, E., et al.: A blockchain and self-sovereign identity empowered digital identity platform. In: 2021 International Conference on Computer Communications and Networks (ICCCN), pp. 1–7. IEEE (2021)

5. Chen, S., et al.: AUSERA: automated security vulnerability detection for android apps. In: 37th IEEE/ACM International Conference on Automated Software Engineering, pp. 1–5 (2022)

6. Chen, Z., et al.: A blockchain-based preserving and sharing system for medical data privacy. Futur. Gener. Comput. Syst. **124**, 338–350 (2021)

7. Enck, W., et al.: TaintDroid: an information-flow tracking system for realtime privacy monitoring on smartphones. ACM Trans. Comput. Syst. (TOCS) **32**(2), 1–29 (2014)

8. Fan, M., et al.: An empirical evaluation of GDPR compliance violations in android mHealth apps. In: 2020 IEEE 31st international symposium on software reliability engineering (ISSRE), pp. 253–264. IEEE (2020)

9. Hankerson, D., et al.: Guide to Elliptic Curve Cryptography. Springer, Heidelberg (2006)

10. Haupert, V., Maier, D., Schneider, N., Kirsch, J., Müller, T.: Honey, i shrunk your app security: the state of android app hardening. In: Giuffrida, C., Bardin, S., Blanc, G. (eds.) DIMVA 2018. LNCS, vol. 10885, pp. 69–91. Springer, Cham (2018). https://doi.org/10.1007/978-3-319-93411-2_4

11. Le, N.T.T., et al.: Assuring non-fraudulent transactions in cash on delivery by introducing double smart contracts. Int. J. Adv. Comput. Sci. Appl. **10**(5), 677–684 (2019)

12. Mia, M.R., et al.: A comparative study on HIPAA technical safeguards assessment of android mHealth applications. Smart Health **26**, 100349 (2022)

13. Sengupta, A., et al.: User control of personal mhealth data using a mobile blockchain app: design science perspective. JMIR mHealth uHealth **10**(1), e32104 (2022)

14. Son, H.X., Carminati, B., Ferrari, E.: A risk assessment mechanism for android apps. In: 2021 IEEE International Conference on Smart Internet of Things (SmartIoT), pp. 237–244. IEEE (2021)

15. Son, H.X., Carminati, B., Ferrari, E.: PriApp-install: learning user privacy preferences on mobile apps' installation. In: Su, C., Gritzalis, D., Piuri, V. (eds.) ISPEC 2022. LNCS, vol. 13620, pp. 306–323. Springer, Cham (2022). https://doi.org/10.1007/978-3-031-21280-2_17

16. Son, H.X., Carminati, B., Ferrari, E.: A risk estimation mechanism for android apps based on hybrid analysis. Data Sci. Eng. **7**(3), 242–252 (2022)

17. Son, H.X., et al.: In2P-med: toward the individual privacy preferences identity in the medical web apps. In: Garrigós, I., Murillo Rodríguez, J.M., Wimmer, M. (eds.) ICWE 2023. LNCS, vol. 13893, pp. 126–140. Springer, Cham (2023). https://doi.org/10.1007/978-3-031-34444-2_10

18. Talha, K.A., et al.: APK auditor: permission-based android malware detection system. Digit. Investig. **13**, 1–14 (2015)

19. Xiao, J., et al.: An android application risk evaluation framework based on minimum permission set identification. J. Syst. Softw. **163**, 110533 (2020)

20. Zhang, H., et al.: Protecting data in android external data storage. In: 2019 IEEE 43rd Annual Computer Software and Applications Conference (COMPSAC), vol. 1, pp. 924–925. IEEE (2019)

21. Zheng, Z., et al.: Blockchain challenges and opportunities: a survey. Int. J. Web Grid Serv. **14**(4), 352–375 (2018)

Application and Industry Track

A Semi-supervised Learning Based Method for Identifying Idle Virtual Machines in Managed Cloud: Application and Practice

Xian Yu[1,2], Kejiang Ye[1], Zihong Chen[2], Jia Yi[2], Xiaofan Chen[2], Bozhong Liu[2], and Chengzhong Xu[1(✉)]

[1] Shenzhen Institute of Advanced Technology, Chinese Academy of Sciences, Shenzhen, China
`kj.ye@siat.ac.cn, czxu@um.edu.mo`
[2] Sangfor Technologies Inc, Shenzhen, China
`{yuxian,yijia29285,chenxiaofan,liubozhong}@sangfor.com.cn`

Abstract. Due to unreasonable virtual machine (VM) resource planning and complex load variation, the waste of VM resource has become a significant issue for many enterprises. Although existing technical solutions have proven to have certain ability to identify idle VMs, most of them are researched in private cloud or public cloud scenarios. And it lacks an effective method customized for managed clouds, where the previous work still suffers from the challenges of fewer labels, poor data quality and large scale of VMs in production environments. For this reason, we first investigate the resource usage data of thousands of VMs from a real managed cloud. Based on the analysis results, we propose an innovative and practical method to identify idle VMs. Through elaborate data processing, feature engineering, and model training, the proposed method enables to achieve excellent performance. Sufficient experiments based on real data from the managed cloud of Sangfor company also prove its practicality and effectiveness in the production environment. Up to now, this service has been deployed in Sangfor cloud for more than 5 months, continuously detecting over 10K VMs, and helping to save at least 1K vCPU cores, 2.5 TB memory and 100 TB disk space.

Keywords: idle virtual machine · machine learning · managed cloud data center · micro-service · random forest model · semi-supervised learning

1 Introduction

Managed cloud is an emerging cloud service mode [1]. It runs as a 2B service mode and serves a wide range of industries, such as education, government, commercial enterprises, etc. The operators of managed cloud provide an exclusive or shared resource pool for those enterprises to choose from. However, due to the

Y. Zhang and L.-J. Zhang (Eds.): ICWS 2023, LNCS 14209, pp. 65–82, 2023.
https://doi.org/10.1007/978-3-031-44836-2_5

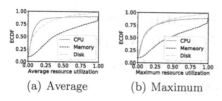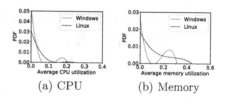

<table>
<tr><td>(a) Average</td><td>(b) Maximum</td><td>(a) CPU</td><td>(b) Memory</td></tr>
</table>

Fig. 1. Empirical cumulative distribution function (ECDF) of resource utilization of approximately 4K VMs in Sangfor cloud.

Fig. 2. Probability density function (PDF) of average resource utilization of 200 idle VMs pre-determined by SREs.

unreasonable allocation and management of Virtual Machines (VMs) by tenants, a large amount of VM resources are wasted, greatly increasing the IT operating costs. For example, some tenants are used to allocate far more resources than they actually need when creating a new VM; software developers may temporarily open multiple VMs for testing purposes, but forget to release them afterwards. Figure 1 shows the resource utilization distribution of CPU, memory and disk of approximately 4K VMs from Sangfor cloud for a week, which owns more than 3000 physical servers and 10000 VMs. The analysis results reveal an extremely serious waste of VM resources in this cloud, especially CPU and disk resources.

To eliminate this problem and provide better cost management services, Site Reliability Engineers (SREs) will regularly clean up the infrequently used VMs or those with long-term low resource occupancy. Unfortunately, when it involves thousands of VMs, manual identifying the idle ones is quite time-consuming and costly. Moreover, the services or processes running on different VMs vary greatly, which makes it be impossible to accurately detect all idle VMs by setting a static threshold or simple rules [2–4]. To be more effective, a functional idle VM detection method is therefore fundamental for managed cloud. Although a large amount of existing work has been proposed to use dynamic thresholds [5], or bring in some machine learning (ML) models [6–9] to learn the variation pattern of the VM resource or performance metrics, these methods either produce too large overhead or require enough positive sample labels, or do not consider the impact of operating system (OS) type on the identification model. Consequently, these methods are hard to be applied to production environment.

To this end, we investigate the application of ML methods in the identification of idle VMs, and present an idle VM identification algorithm based on the Random Forest model [10] and the corresponding micro-service deployment framework. The entire study is conducted on Sangfor cloud, and the service has been successfully deployed for a period of time. We first elaborately perform feature engineering to improve the accuracy and efficiency of idle VM detection by referring to the daily experience of SRE in identifying idle VMs. We then experimentally compare various prevalent ML models and select the best one as the final model to detect idle VMs. Interestingly, we train two detection models separately depending on the type of VM OS (Linux and windows). Consider-

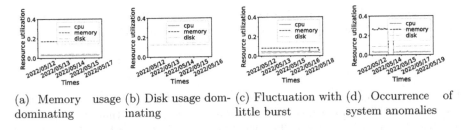

(a) Memory usage dominating (b) Disk usage dominating (c) Fluctuation with little burst (d) Occurrence of system anomalies

Fig. 3. Typical resource usage patterns of idle VMs.

ing the labor-intensive labeling work, we also present a semi-supervised learning algorithm to help train the model, in which we particularly propose a sample augmentation algorithm to address the problem of insufficient positive samples. We conduct plenty of online data exception handling, so as to reduce the influence of data quality on identification results. Last but not least, the implementation of the entire system follows the principle of micro-service design, where the idle VM identification model runs stateless and retrain periodically, which facilitates rapid online expansion and update after deployment.

The contributions of this paper include:

- We analyze real VM resource occupancy data and design 15 kinds of key time-series features to detect idle VMs, and we also find that idle VMs installed with Linux generally have lower memory occupancy than idle VMs installed with windows.
- We investigate in depth how to identify idle VMs using resource metrics of VMs along with ML models, and propose a practical and lightweight idle VM detection method based on random forest-based model, as well as the corresponding micro-service detection framework.
- The proposed method has been applied to the production environment for several months, and the results of a large number of offline experiments and online service running data prove its effectiveness and efficiency.

The following paper is organized as follows. We first introduce the motivation and challenges of this work in Sect. 2, and propose a ML-based idle VM detection method in Sect. 3. We evaluate the proposed method in Sect. 4. We further analyze its performance and overhead after it is deployed to production environment in Sect. 5. Some related work is described in Sect. 6. We state the limitations of this work in Sect. 7 and draw a conclusion in Sect. 8.

2   Background

Idle VMs in this work refer to inactive VMs (or sprawled [11]), not just that it is not running any user programs. We expect to find idle VMs by analyzing their resource or performance indicators, which can be used as a basis for shrinking their capacity or closing them to save costs. In this section, we begin by presenting several findings from the analysis of VM resource usage data. The analysis results serve as the main motivation for our method. Next, we summarize the main challenges of solving this problem in a production environment.

2.1   Observations

In order to better understand the characteristics of idle VMs, SREs randomly select several VMs in advance, and manually label 200 VMs that they think are idle based on their experience. Two thirds of these VMs have linux OS installed and the remaining have windows OS installed. We analyze the resource usage of all these idle VMs and make the following two findings.

- **Observation I:** The resource utilization of idle VMs running linux significantly differs from that of idle VMs running windows. We compare the average CPU and memory resource utilization distributions of idle VMs with windows and linux. The statistical probability density distribution (PDF) results are displayed in Fig. 2. According to the results, we can find that the average resource utilization of idle VMs with linux presents a long-tail distribution, while that of idle VMs with windows show an obvious crest change. This change may be caused by two types of windows services, Virtual Desktop Infrastructure (VDI) service [12] and traditional office service. The difference in resource distribution between VMs with windows and linux leads to the need for a differentiated model to identify idle VMs with different types of OS.
- **Observation II:** Idle VMs have similar patterns of resource usage and variation. Figure 3 shows four typical resource usage trends of idle VMs. Figure 3(a) and Fig. 3(b) respectively represent idle VMs dominated by memory occupancy and disk occupancy, and the curves are relatively stable. Figure 3(c) shows that the resource occupancy curve of idle VM fluctuates with little burst, and Fig. 3(d) indicates the idle VM is experiencing some kind of anomalies. Note that these idle VMs are manually marked by SREs, which means SREs believe that the resource occupancy of a idle VM should be similar to these patterns. We further analyze the commonalities between these patterns and find that all VMs labeled as idle by SREs generally have low resource utilization (CPU utilization, memory utilization, and disk utilization in Fig. 3 are all below 30%). Moreover, all these curves are not consistently volatile. These findings show the major differences between idle and non-idle VMs and become the primary basis for determining whether a VM is idle.

2.2   Challenges

Although a large amount of methods [2–5, 13–15] have been proposed to detect inactive VMs, these methods are rarely applied to real production environments. For better application performance in the production environment, we summarize several key challenges that require to be broken through.

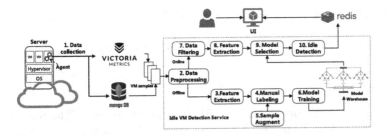

Fig. 4. The proposed idle VMs detection framework.

- **Challenge I: High performance.** A key point to accurately identify idle VMs through ML models is to select appropriate VM resource features. Although there are some public libraries (e.g. tsfresh [16]) that can extract thousands of temporal features , these features not only cause a large extraction overhead, but also requires sufficient samples to ensure the success of model training. More importantly, labeling the idle VMs is very time-consuming, some supervised classification models is thus unable to be applied directly, which further increases the difficulty of identifying idle VMs.
- **Challenge II: Lightweight design.** Unlike large-scale public cloud environments, the available resources in managed cloud environments are insufficient, which requires the designed detection method to be as lightweight as possible. Although the detection speed can be improved by multi-process or multi-threading techniques, these methods also bring about extra resource cost. As a result, the current outstanding large neural network models [17,18] are difficult to be practically applied to addressing this problem, which is also the main reason for this work focusing on the classical ML models.
- **Challenge III: Robust and extensible framework.** For one thing, the idle VM identification method needs to be able to proactively detect and eliminate online data quality problems caused by potential bugs, design defects and irregular updates and upgrades of the monitoring system, as well as the network congestion and device failure. For another thing, it also needs to automatically recognize some long-term holidays (e.g., China's National Day, Spring Festival) to avoid false positives. Furthermore, the design of this detection service must be stateless for a highly scalable capability to better adapt to large-scale VM scaling scenarios.

We set out how to solve above challenges in following Sect. 3.

3   Proposed Method

In this section, we propose a ML model based and micro-service framework to address the challenges mentioned above. Section 3.1 depicts an overview of the proposed idle VM detection framework. We introduce the metrics used to detect idle VMs in Sect. 3.2. We describe the extracted key features from these metrics in Sect. 3.3. A probabilistic idle VM detection model and the associated semi-supervised training algorithm are respectively presented in Sect. 3.4 and Sect. 3.5. We state how to detect and deal with idle VMs in Sect. 3.6.

3.1   Overview

Figure 4 displays the proposed idle VM detection framework. The relevant data used to detect idle VMs will first be uploaded through the agent deployed in the VM. Static VM information will be stored in a configuration management database (CMDB), and other time series data (such as CPU utilization, memory utilization) will be stored in a time series database (TSDB). The idle VM detection service will pull these data to complete offline training and online detection.

The training phase is composed of step 2 to step 6. In this phase, the VM data will first undergo noise reduction and normalization, and then will be transformed into feature vectors. The feature vectors will be used as the input of the detection model. After that, SREs will manually mark few positive and negative samples. Based on these samples, this idle VM detection service will automatically generate more samples through the presented sample augmentation algorithm to improve the generalization capability. The trained model will be stored in the model warehouse and updated periodically. The phase of online detection mainly corresponds to step 7 to step 10, where the detection service regularly pulls the VM data and make identification. It will first preprocess the input data and further filter out those during a long-term holiday or in the agent upgrade stage. Next, it extracts the idle features and selects the appropriate model for detection based on the type of VM OS. The detection results will be updated to UI interface, and users can perform different treatments according to the detection results and mark the detected VMs as correct or incorrect. The feedback will be converted into training samples to participate in the next model update.

3.2   VM Data Collection

We mainly choose three VM resource indicators to detect idle VMs, including CPU utilization, memory utilization, and disk utilization. Unlike some previous researches, in addition to selecting these resource indicators, they also consider several more complex indicators, such as network connection, application-related system calls and key service processes. The main reason why we only select these indicators is to consider that the current user needs are mainly concerned with these types of VM resources, and the use of these indicators is more in line with the manual identification habits of SRE personnel. Moreover, too many features will not only cause high collection overhead, but also easily lead to degradation of detection efficiency. Note that our method is also suitable for rapid expansion and application to other metric data. Besides, we also collect the indicators of system uptime and the number of keyboard and mouse operations for those VMs with windows OS. These metrics are beneficial to compensate for the shortcomings of the ML-based detection model through several predefined rules.

To obtain these VM indicator data, we developed an agent that runs in VM in the form of a process and uploads the relevant data in real time. When collecting these data of tenant's VMs, we will strictly abide by the negotiation agreement with tenant, so there will be no data privacy issues.

3.3   Determining Idle Features

Although we have reduced the complexity of idle VM detection to a certain extent by controlling the number of participating detection indicators, due to the diversity of time series, each VM resource indicator can still extract up to thousands of features, which will inevitably lead to high performance loss and time overhead. Based on the observation 2 mentioned in Sect. 2.1, we summarize two kinds of key features for detecting idle VMs: statistical features and fluctuating features. In particular, we screen out 9 basic statistical features and 6 time-series fluctuation features from more than 1,000 features generated by tsfresh [16] through correlation test, variance test, and P-value test. The information description of the extracted features can be found in Table 1, and their detailed calculation process can refer to tsfresh [16].

Table 1. The extracted features from each kind of VM resource utilization sequence.

Categories	Feature names	Description
Basic statistical features	Minimum	The minimum value of the sequence.
	Maximum	The maximum value of the sequence.
	Mean	The mean of the sequence.
	Median	The median of the sequence.
	Variance	The variance of the sequence.
	Standard deviation	The standard deviation of the sequence.
	Root mean square	The root mean square of the VM resource utilization sequence.
	Var larger than std	A boolean value indicating whether the variance of the sequence is greater than the standard deviation of it.
	Ratio larger than mean	The proportion of the objects that are greater than the mean value in the sequence.
Sequence fluctuation features	Variation coefficient	The discrete degree of the sequence calculated under a unified numerical dimension.
	Sample entropy	Measuring the probability of generating new patterns in the sequence.
	Permutation entropy	Quantitative assessment of random noise contained in the sequence.
	Binned entropy	The binned entropy of the power spectral density of the sequence.
	Complexity invariant distance	The degree of chaos in the sequence.
	Absolute sum of changes	The magnitude of the change in the sequence.

3.4   Detection Model Design

Intuitively, idle VM detection is a 0–1 binary classification problem. However, directly determining whether a VM is idle may confuse SREs, so that it is impossible to make the best disposal action. The main reason for this confusion is that the so-called idle VM also needs to consider issues such as idle time period and idle degree. Therefore, to eliminate this confusion, we turn this problem into a detection probability problem. Specifically, we define an idle probability P to indicate how likely a VM to be idle. In fact, we also predefined a set of idle probability thresholds, each of which corresponds to a different processing method for idle VMs (such as resource scaling, shutdown, etc.). The formal mathematical expression for this detection process is as follows:

$$P(V_k) = Func(\overrightarrow{f_{V_k}^1}, \overrightarrow{f_{V_k}^2}, \ldots, \overrightarrow{f_{V_k}^N})$$

where $f_{V_k}^i$ means the extracted feature vector of i-th indicator of VM V_k. Although many deep learning models have been widely used in image recognition [17], text classifications [18], they will also bring huge training and prediction costs. For this reason,our work concentrates on the classical ML models. After evaluating 10 kinds of ML models, and considering that the Random Forest (RF) model [10] naturally conforms to the characteristics of probability selection, we finally chose it to detect idle VMs. Moreover, RF model has a recognized good

---

Algorithm 1. An automated sample augmentation algorithm

Input: The mean distribution (λ_m^k) and the deviation distribution (λ_d^k) of k-th indicator of labeled idle VM samples, total number of generated samples (N), total number of indicators (M) and the length of generated indicator series (L)

Output: New generated idle VM sample set (Θ)

1: Set $i, k \leftarrow 0$;
2: Sampling function Φ;
3: **while** $i \leq N$ **do**
4:     Initiate a new null sample θ_i;
5:     **while** $k \leq M$ **do**
6:        Generate an equivalent sequence s_i^k with length of L, $s_i^k[0:L] \leftarrow \Phi_1(\lambda_m^k)$;
7:        Update $s_i^k \leftarrow s_i^k + \Phi_L(\lambda_d^k)$;
8:        Update $s_i^k \leftarrow s_i^k + \Phi_L(\mathcal{N}(0, \sigma^2))$;
9:        **if** $\Phi_1(\mathcal{U}(0,1)) \leq p$ **then**
10:           New variables $x_1, x_2 \leftarrow \lfloor(\Phi_2(\mathcal{U}(0, L)))\rfloor$;
11:           Set $s_i^k[min(x_1,x_2) : max(x_1,x_2)] \leftarrow 0$;
12:        **end if**
13:        Add s_i^k to sample θ_i;
14:        $k \leftarrow k + 1$;
15:     **end while**
16:     Add θ_i to sample set Θ;
17:     $i \leftarrow i + 1$;
18: **end while**

---

interpretability, which is very friendly for users. Detailed experimental comparisons between different models can be found in Sect. 4.

3.5   Semi-supervised Training

Labeling VM as idle is actually a very labor-intensive task, which leads to a lack of positive samples, that is, the samples marked as idle. Consequently, the trained detection model tends to identify VMs as active, resulting in a low precision. To address this issue, we propose an empirical sample augmentation algorithm to automatically generate idle VM samples. The core principle of this algorithm is to generate new samples after certain data perturbation on the basis of the original marked sample data distribution. The pseudo code of the algorithm is shown in Algorithm 1.

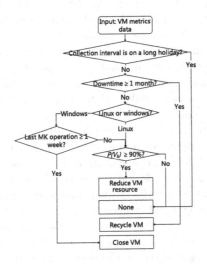

Fig. 5. Procedure of detecting and recommended dispose of idle VMs.

The input of this algorithm mainly includes: The mean distribution (λ_m^k) and the deviation distribution (λ_d^k) of k-th indicator, which are derived from manually labeled idle VM sample data; Total number of generated samples (N), total number of indicators (M) for identifying idle VMs and the length of generated indicator series (L). This algorithm outputs newly generated idle VM samples. For each indicator in any newly generated sample, this algorithm first produces an equivalent sequence s_i^k with length of L based on the mean distribution λ_m^k (Line 1–6). The symbol of $\Phi_l(\lambda)$ in Algorithm 1 represents the random generation of l values based on the distribution λ. It then superimposes on the sequence s_i^k a deviation sequence randomly generated according to the distribution λ_d^k (Line 7). In order to enhance the generalization ability of trained model, we superimposes on the sequence s_i^k a noise sequence randomly generated according to a normal distribution of $\mathcal{N}(0, \sigma^2)$ (Line 8). Besides, we further select a continuous partial sequence from the sequence s_i^k and set its value as 0, which is used to simulate the actual data loss caused by machine failure and system upgrade (Line 9–12). The generated data is then gradually added to the sample set Θ (Line 13–17). The parameters of σ and p are set to 0.002 and 0.01 respectively.

After generating enough training and testing samples, we adopt 10-fold cross validation method to train the model. It should be emphasized that the samples detected online and marked by users will also be regularly added to the training set to improve the accuracy of the model.

3.6   Online Detection

According to long-term observation, we find that changes such as system upgrade and network adjustment occasionally occur in the production environment. It will lead to the loss of a large amount of monitoring data, and misleads the model to mistakenly identify active VMs as idle, resulting in large false positives. To distinguish the data loss caused by such large-scale changes from the data loss caused by small-range equipment failures, we define a support degree q to represent the proportion of VMs that lose data in the same time period. If q is greater than a predetermined threshold (such as 60%), events such as batch system upgrade are considered to occur in the production environment with a high probability. In this case, the detection service will directly filter out these loss data, that is, they will not participate in the detection process.

To facilitate SRE to handle the identified idle VMs, we not only use the predicted results of the detection model, but also design some rules based on the on/off state of the VM and the operation of the mouse and keyboard (MK operation) to comprehensively decide the disposal method for idle VMs. The detailed design is shown in Fig. 5. We will first simply ignore to detect those VMs that are in the long holiday period, such as National Day, Labor Day. Next, we will continue to judge the online duration of the VM. If the VM has been shut down for more than one month, we will regard it as a zombie VM and recommend recycling it directly. Otherwise, we will use the trained model to further infer whether the VM is idle. If $P(V_k)$ is greater than or equal to 90%, we believe that this VM has a high probability of being inactive, and recommend reducing its allocated resources. Note that we have added an additional judgment rule for those VMs with windows OS, that is, if the VM has not been operated through the keyboard and mouse for more than a week, we consider this VM to be inactive, and recommend shutting it down. All threshold parameters mentioned in Fig. 5 can be adjusted according to actual requirements.

4   Experiment and Evaluation

For comprehensively evaluating the effectiveness of IdleVMDetector, we first conduct a large number of experiments in an offline environment. In these experiments, we not only compare the impact of selecting different ML models on performance and overhead, but also illustrate the benefits of our proposed feature engineering technique and sample enhancement algorithm.

4.1 Experimental Setup

We totally compare 10 different popular ML models: Decision Tree (DT), Bagging, AdaBoost, Gradient Boosting Decision Tree (GBDT), Random Forest (RF), Support Vector Classification (SVC) with rbf kernel, Logistic Regression (LR), and 3 kinds of Multilayer Perceptron (MLP) models. MLP(a, b) means the model has b layers of neural networks, and each layer has a neurons. All these models are implemented by python-3.8.4 and sk-learn library [19]. The training set consists of 45 manually labeled positive samples (idle VMs), 65 negative samples (busy VMs), and 500 samples generated by the proposed sample augmentation algorithm. We also generate 500 labeled VMs for validation. Considering the high labor costs, these idle and busy VMs are determined by IT personnel purely based on their historical resource usage. That is, these labels do not really reflect whether these VMs is being used. Therefore, we generate additional 500 labeled samples to participate in the validation set to improve the accuracy of the evaluation. The performance metrics used in this work include: precision, recall and F1-Score, which have been widely used in various classification problems. The overhead indicators include time consumption of model training and prediction, as well as the resource occupancy when running online.

All experiments are conducted in a VM by taking use of 2 processes. The VM is configured with 8 CPU cores and 16G memory. The configuration of each CPU core is Intel(R) Xeon(R) Gold 5220R CPU @ 2.20GHz. To eliminate the influence of experimental error, each experiment is repeated by 10 times.

Table 2. Performance and time overhead comparison of IdleVMDetector using different ML models (The model we finally adopt is highlighted in red).

Evaluation metrics	DT	Bagging	AdaBoost	BGDT	RF	SVC	LR	MLP-(50, 1)	MLP-(50, 2)	MLP-(50, 3)
Precision	0.929	0.931	0.935	0.938	0.946	0.784	0.900	0.897	0.870	0.855
Recall	0.928	0.932	0.941	0.936	0.941	0.934	0.971	0.897	0.903	0.912
F1-Score	0.928	0.932	0.938	0.937	0.944	0.852	0.934	0.896	0.883	0.882
Average training time (s)	0.011	0.066	0.199	0.677	0.094	0.021	0.066	0.628	0.700	0.994
Average prediction time (s)	0.003	0.009	0.028	0.004	0.008	0.052	0.003	0.003	0.003	0.011

4.2 Comparison Between ML Models

Table 4 shows the performance and overhead of the selected 10 kinds of ML models in identifying idle VMs. The experimental results show that the f1-score of the tree-based models (DT, Bagging, AdaBoost and GBT) is better than that of SVC and MLP models. The main reason for this phenomenon is that the features selected by our feature engineering are relatively independent, which is more suitable for tree-structured models to learn. That is also why LR model enables to achieve better F1-Score performance than SVC and MLP. On the contrary, SVC and MLP models will comprehensively consider the correlation between different features, leading to learning some irrelevant knowledge. Among these tree-based models, RF slightly outperforms other models (1% $\sim$ 3%), and considering that the average time consumption of a single prediction of RF is extremely low (≤ 10 ms), we finally choose RF to detect idle VMs.

4.3 The Impact of Feature Engineering

According to the experimental results in Fig. 6, the efficiency of feature extraction, training, and prediction has been significantly improved after feature engineering. Among them, the time consumption of single feature extraction and prediction is reduced by nearly 65.2% compared to that before feature engineering. The reason for such progress is that a large number of useless features are eliminated through feature engineering, that is, only 15 of the original 2361 features are retained. More importantly, from Fig. 6(a), we can find that the removal of 99.4% features has little impact on the performance, and F1-Score drop rate is less than 1% after feature engineering. This is a good news for us and is within our expectations, because removing features also means that some valuable underlying information may be eliminated. It also proves that the feature engineering we have carried out not only improves the detection efficiency, but also preserves the valuable information in the original data as much as possible.

4.4 The Impact of Sample Augmentation Algorithm

Figure 7 shows the curve of the performance of IdleVMDetector changing with the number of constructed samples. When the number of newly generated samples is less than 1000, the detection performance improves significantly with the increase of the number of samples, the F1-Score of which is improved by about 17% compared to the model directly trained without generating any samples. The main reason for this improvement is that the newly generated samples not only solve the imbalance problem between positive and negative samples in the training process, but also expand the sample knowledge boundary that the model can learn, thus greatly improving the generalization ability of the model. This is also why the sample augmentation algorithm improves the performance of recall more significantly than the performance of accuracy. After the number of samples exceeds 1000, the marginal effect of the new knowledge that the model can learn decreases, so the detection performance gradually tends to be stable.

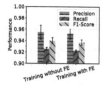
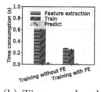
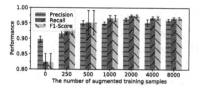

(a) Performance   (b) Time overhead

Fig. 6. Comparison of effect on whether IdleVMDetector uses feature engineering (FE) techniques.

Fig. 7. Impact of the number of augmented training samples on detection performance.

5   Implementation and Deployment

Considering that there are over 10K VMs in production environment, we have taken use of multi-process technology to improve the detection efficiency, and the entire service is packaged separately into a container image, managed by K8s [20], so as to ensure high scalability. In the process of interacting with the front-end, we also bring in the technique of asynchronous data transmission. The detection results will first be cached into Redis [21], and the front-end does not directly request the results from the detection service, but reads it from Redis. In order to assist SRE confirm the detection results, the front-end interface also provides some other statistical information of VM resources. The final interface interaction effect of our service is shown in Fig. 8.

We randomly record the results of one detection to introduce the effect of this service in production environment, where the number of configured process and the hardware configuration of the server are the same as the experimental configuration in Sect. 4.1. A total of nearly 3000 VMs are detected in this process, and among these detected VMs, only those VMs (133 VMs in total) with an identified idle probability greater than 95% are taken for disposal. All the detailed analysis results are presented in the following sections.

5.1   Performance Analysis

Table 3 shows 5 kinds of methods for handling the identified idle VMs. The results show that among all 133 identified idle VMs, 71.5% of the VMs have actually been dealt with, including 62.6% of VMs have been de-allocated, 2.2% have been shut down, 6.7% have been recycled. In addition, 16.5% of the VMs are not confirmed whether they really need to be handled due to user-related problems. The remaining 12% of the VMs have not been executed any action, because they all have special individual circumstances, for example, some VMs are newly created, so that their resources should remain unchanged in the short term. We summarize 6 typical scenarios where idle VMs should not be handled, as shown in Table 4. In fact, these idle VMs can be filtered out through the black

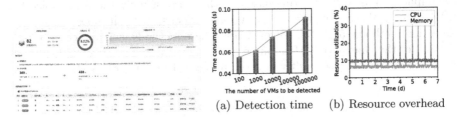

Fig. 8. An example of the effect of our idle VM detection service running online.

Fig. 9. Analysis of IdleVMDetector in production environment.

(a) Detection time   (b) Resource overhead

and white list mechanism before service detection. Overall, these results strongly demonstrate the effectiveness of our proposed idle VM detection method.

5.2 Efficiency and Overhead Analysis

Figure 9(a) and Fig. 9(b) respectively show the change of detection time of IdleVMDetector as the VM increases and the resource overhead of running for a period of time. The results in 9(a) prove that the detection time spent by our method shows a linear growth trend with the expansion of the scale of VMs, so that it can be effectively extended to larger cloud environments. As we expected, the resource utilization of the service during running process shows obvious periodicity, and the peak of the resource utilization curve corresponds to the interval for performing idle VM detection. As shown in Fig. 9(b), the CPU resources and memory resources occupied by the service when detecting tens of thousands of VMs per round are less than 20% and 30% respectively, which satisfy the resource occupation requirements we have set in advance.

6   Related Work

The idle VM identification methods can be classified into two categories: Rule-based method and ML-based method. The former set several rules (or annotations) to identify idle VMs, and the latter takes use of several machine learning algorithms to train a model based on the predefined indicators' features, and use this trained model to infer whether a VM is idle.

Rule-Based Method: Early work identifies idle VMs by intuitively setting a static threshold [2,4] or a simple rule [3]. PULSAR [4] only considers the CPU resource of a VM when identifying this VM as an idle VM, and as long as the CPU resource of this VM is lower than a predefined certain threshold. Snadpiper [2] determines idle VM by extending one kind of VM resource into a combination of three utilization factors (CPU, memory, network usage). Differing from PULSAR and Snadpiper, the work [3] directly recognize the earliest instance as inactive when the utilization of data center is low enough. Due to its nature of simplicity and intuition, rule-based methods are usually the first choice for SREs. This is also the main reason why some recent works still choose rule-based detection methods [5,13,15]. Nevertheless, these methods lack an accurate perception of the change of VM resource occupancy, leading to varying degrees of false negatives and false positives in the process of judging idle VMs.

Table 3. Disposition methods actually performed for identified idle VMs.

Disposition methods	Resource degradation	Shutdown	Resource recycling	Do nothing	Unknown
Proportions	62.6%	2.2%	6.7%	12.0%	16.5%

Table 4. Several typical scenarios of idle VMs that cannot be disposed of.

Categories	Explanation
New environment	Newly purchased and deployed VMs by users.
Resource redundancy	Some VMs need to ensure sufficient resources to meet sudden business loads.
Load balance	The VMs adjusted by the load balancing mechanism.
Authorization requirement	The authorization of some application software is affected by the configured resource size.
System configuration requirement	The VMs that deploy distributed applications, such as Redis or Message Queue.
Test environment	The User Acceptance Test environment needs to be consistent with the user environment.

ML-Based Method: Compared to rule-based methods, ML-based methods provide a more powerful ability to learn VM behavior and its resource variation patterns. The work in [14] leverage kinds of primitive information (e.g., running process, login history, network connections) and a linear support vector machine (SVM) to find the fingerprints of inactive VMs. To better identify cloud garbage instances, the authors in [22] argue that simply using resource metrics to make judgments may be misleading, and then bring in a a weighted reference model based on application information to capture dependency information between users and cloud instances. The iCSI system [6] combines rule-based approaches and ML based approaches to improve the accuracy of idle VM identification. It also chooses SVM as the basic learning model, and additionally adds several judging rules based on the analysis of VM functions and VM network affinity analysis. The work [7] detect underutilized VM through comparing the results of weighted ensemble resource predictions with a predefined threshold. The authors in [8] compare various statistical metrics of all performance data with repeatedly tuned threshold coming from a decision tree learning algorithm to identify idle VM by producing an idleness score. Other researchers in [9] believe that idle VMs should have similar resource change patterns, and they thus propose a clustering method to determine idle VMs based on the VM resource utilization metrics.

Although we also adopt a ML model to infer idle probability, the biggest difference from the existing work is that they do not consider the lack of idle VM labels in real situations, making them difficult to be widely used. Moreover, we train different detection models for different types of VM OS. This is also not considered in the previous work.

7   Limitation

This work starts from the perspective of VM resource occupancy and aims to take use of the relevant metrics to indirectly infer whether VMs are inactive. During online detection process, the proposed system also utilizes some VM running status metrics, such as VM startup duration and the number of key-and-mouse operations, to improve decision-making efficiency. The proposed method conforms to the manual detection idea of SREs. We do not consider the business behavior characteristics of VMs (e.g. VM access relationship, TCP or UDP connections, and process remote calls), which will lead to some network resource-intensive VMs being misreported. Besides, our study focuses on resource usage rather than real business load, and therefore does not consider metrics that is able to more accurately reflect VM service load, such as disk IOPS or business-related system calls. Despite the fact that this proposed method does not take these factors into account, they can be easily extended by drawing into relevant metric data, which is also one of the main goals of our future work.

8   Conclusion

This paper systematically proposes a lightweight idle VM identification method based on a ML model. The proposed method has been successfully applied to a real cloud network environment. This method focuses on analyzing the relationship between the variation pattern of VM resource occupancy and idle status. Based on the observations from real VM data, we design 9 basic statistical features and 6 sequence fluctuation features, and bring in RF model to identify idle VMs. We present a sample augmentation algorithm to solve the problem of lack of positive samples, and introduce several online detection optimization strategies to improve the accuracy and robustness of identifying idle VMs. More importantly, we also summarize 6 scenarios where idle VMs unable to be processed, and further provide some thoughts on optimizing the accuracy of idle VM detection, which will also be the main point in our future work.

This system is deployed in the form of micro-services. Sufficient experiments demonstrate the effectiveness of our proposed idle VM detection method. The system has been running online for several months, showing excellent performance and has helped Sangfor cloud to save large VM resources by far.

Acknowledgment. This work was supported by Cloud Security Key Technology Research Key Laboratory of Shenzhen under grant No.ZDSY20200811143600002, the National Key R&D Program of China (No. 2021YFB3300200), National Natural Science Foundation of China (No. 62072451, 92267105), Guangdong Special Support Plan (No. 2021TQ06X990), and Shenzhen Basic Research Program (No. JCYJ20200109115418592, JCYJ20220818101610023). We would like to express thanks to the reviewers and editors for their constructive comments and suggestions. We also thank anyone who helped us improve this work.

References

1. Insight, Managed cloud services. https://www.insight.com/en_US/glossary/m/managed-cloud-services.html (2022)
2. Wood, T., Shenoy, P., Venkataramani, A., Yousif, M.: Black-box and gray-box strategies for virtual machine migration. In: NSDI, vol. 7, pp. 17–17 (2007)
3. Calheiros, R.N., Ranjan, R., Buyya, R.: Virtual machine provisioning based on analytical performance and QOS in cloud computing environments. In: 2011 International Conference on Parallel Processing. IEEE, 2011, pp. 295–304 (2011)
4. Breitgand, D., et al.: An adaptive utilization accelerator for virtualized environments. In: 2014 IEEE International Conference on Cloud Engineering. IEEE, 2014, pp. 165–174 (2014)
5. Chunlin, L., Hammad-Ur-Rehman, Q.: Adaptive threshold detection based on current demand for efficient utilization of cloud resources. In: 2019 IEEE 4th International Conference on Computer and Communication Systems (ICCCS). IEEE, 2019, pp. 341–346 (2019)
6. IKim, I.K., Zeng, S., Young, C., Hwang, J., Humphrey, M.: iCSI: A cloud garbage VM collector for addressing inactive VMs with machine learning. In: 2017 IEEE International Conference on Cloud Engineering (IC2E) (2017)
7. Mazidi, A., Mahdavi, M., Roshanfar, F.: An autonomic decision tree-based and deadline-constraint resource provisioning in cloud applications. Concurr. Comput.: Pract. Exp. **33**(10), e6196 (2021)
8. Khandros, M., et al.: Machine learning computing model for virtual machine underutilization detection. Jul. 6 2021, uS Patent 11,055,126 (2021)
9. Gopisetti, A., Jha, C., George, J.R., Gaurav, K., Singh, J.: Usage pattern virtual machine idle detection. Feb. 10 2022, uS Patent App. 17/510,546
10. Breiman, L.: Random forests. Mach. Learn. **45**(1), 5–32 (2001)
11. Lindner, M., McDonald, F., McLarnon, B., Robinson, P.: Towards automated business-driven indication and mitigation of vm sprawl in cloud supply chains. In: 12th IFIP/IEEE International Symposium on Integrated Network Management (IM: and Workshops. IEEE 2011, pp. 1062–1065 (2011)
12. Microsoft Azure, What is virtual desktop infrastructure (vdi)? https://azure.microsoft.com/en-us/resources/cloud-computing-dictionary/what-is-virtual-desktop-infrastructure-vdi/ (2022)
13. Fesl, J., Gokhale, V., Feslová, M.: Efficient virtual machine consolidation approach based on user inactivity detection. Cloud Comput. **2019**, 115 (2019)
14. Kim, I.K., Zeng, S., Young, C., Hwang, J., Humphrey, M.: A supervised learning model for identifying inactive vms in private cloud data centers. In: Proceedings of the Industrial Track of the 17th International Middleware Conference, 2016, pp. 1–7 (2016)
15. Zhang, B., Al Dhuraibi, Y., Rouvoy, R., Paraiso, F., Seinturier, L.: Cloudgc: Recycling idle virtual machines in the cloud. In: 2017 IEEE International Conference on Cloud Engineering (IC2E). IEEE, 2017, pp. 105–115 (2017)
16. Christ, M., Braun, N., Neuffer, J., Kempa-Liehr, A.W., et al.: Tsfresh. https://tsfresh.readthedocs.io/en/latest/text/introduction.html (2022)
17. Li, Y.: Research and application of deep learning in image recognition. In: 2022 IEEE 2nd International Conference on Power, Electronics and Computer Applications (ICPECA). IEEE, 2022, pp. 994–999 (2022)
18. Li, Q., et al.: A survey on text classification: from traditional to deep learning. ACM Trans. Intell. Syst. Technol. (TIST) **13**(2), 1–41 (2022)

19. Scikit-learn.org: Scikit-learn. https://scikit-learn.org/stable/ (2022)
20. Kubernetes Enterprise: Kubernetes (k8s). https://kubernetes.io/ (2022)
21. Redis Enterprise: Reids. https://redis.io/ (2022)
22. Shen, Z., Young, C.C., Zeng, S., Murthy, K., Bai, K.: Identifying resources for cloud garbage collection. In: 2016 12th International Conference on Network and Service Management (CNSM) (2016)

MyKSC: Disaggregated Containerized Supercomputer Platform

Ju-Won Park[✉][iD], Joon Woo, and Taeyoung Hong

Korea Institute of Science and Technology Information,
245 Daehak-ro, Daejeon 34141, Republic of Korea
{juwon.park,wjnadia,tyhong}@kisti.re.kr

Abstract. Recently, with the emergence of cloud-based machine learning application services such as ChatGPT and big data analytics, which require high-volume data learning, demand for large-scale high-performance computing (HPC) resources has significantly increased. However, there are many difficulties in providing cloud-based services owing to the differences in existing HPC resource operation and execution environments. To address these challenges, there are many ongoing research efforts to support cloud application services on HPC systems using container technology. However, there are fundamental differences between traditional HPC and cloud applications that make administrators hesitant to adopt them in actual operating environments. To solve these problems, this paper introduces MyKSC, which provides a unified user interface based on a loosely-coupled architecture. MyKSC is a system applied to Nurion, a supercomputer operated by the Korean National Supercomputing Center (KISTI). Nurion users can use new cloud application services such as Jupyter and RStudio along with existing HPC application services like MPI through MyKSC. To achieve this, MyKSC divides the entire system into Kubernetes and HPC clusters and selects suitable cluster resources to run the application based on user preferences. This paper proposes the loosely-coupled containerized supercomputer platform and introduces its current implementation.

Keywords: Loosely-coupled · containerization · unified interface

1 Introduction

Recently, with the emergence of cloud-based machine learning application services such as ChatGPT and big data analytics, which require high-volume data learning, the demand for large-scale high-performance computing (HPC) resources has significantly increased. However, supporting cloud application services through existing HPC resources is challenging owing to the rigid software stack [8,13]. Container technology can be a very good alternative to solving

This work was supported by the Korea Institute of Science and Technology Information (Grant No. K-23-L02-C01-S01).

Y. Zhang and L.-J. Zhang (Eds.): ICWS 2023, LNCS 14209, pp. 83–91, 2023.
https://doi.org/10.1007/978-3-031-44836-2_6

these problems. Because it shows very good performance through a lightweight virtualization layer, many studies are being conducted to introduce container technology in the HPC field [3,4,9]. However, despite these efforts, there are restrictions due to fundamental differences between typical HPC and cloud applications, including resource utilization, the scale of tasks and service execution times, and the way services are executed.

To solve these problems, this paper introduces MyKSC, which provides a unified user interface based on a loosely-coupled architecture. MyKSC is a system applied to Nurion, a supercomputer operated by KISTI. Nurion users can use new cloud application services such as Jupyter and RStudio along with existing HPC application services like MPI through MyKSC. MyKSC divides the entire system into a Kubernetes cluster for providing cloud application services and a traditional scheduler-based HPC cluster. Based on these divided resources, MyKSC selects suitable cluster resources to run the application depending on the type of service chosen by the user. That is, new cloud application services such as Jupyter and RStudio are executed on the Kubernetes cluster, while for traditional HPC applications, it generates a job script file based on user interaction (e.g., file selection, parameter input) and submits it to the existing HPC cluster's batch job scheduler to perform the actual task on the HPC cluster.

The remainder of this paper is organized as follows. Section 2 introduces Nurion and related studies. In Sect. 3, we present the architecture of the proposed platform. We next present the implementation of MyKSC in Sect. 4. Finally, we present our conclusions in Sect. 5.

2   Background

2.1   Specifications and Structure of the 5th Supercomputer

Nurion is the 5th HPC system built by the Korean National Supercomputing Center (KISTI) in 2018. It is a cluster system consisting of 8,305 Intel Xeon Phi-based KNL CPU nodes and 132 Intel Xeon SKL CPU nodes, with a theoretical performance of 25.7 *PFlops*. The user data are stored in a 20 *PBytes* Lustre parallel file system, and all compute nodes and parallel file systems are connected with a 100 *Gbps* omni-path architecture (OPA) interconnector that provides ultra-high-speed/low-latency communication. Nurion provides users with two personal folders: (*/scratch*) and (*/home*). */home* provides 64 GB of storage space for user-specific data and has no file deletion policy. By contrast, */scratch* is a temporary storage space for all files needed for task execution: it provides up to 100 TB of space but automatically deletes unused files every 15 days. To prevent performance degradation in the parallel file system, a burst buffer was introduced. The burst buffer is a cache layer for I/O acceleration between compute nodes and storage, preventing performance degradation due to small I/O or random I/O in the parallel file system and maximizing parallel I/O performance. In addition, Nurion uses the portable batch system (PBS) as the batch job scheduler for workload management, and an exclusive node allocation policy is applied by default to ensure that only one user's task can be executed per node to guarantee the maximum application performance.

2.2   Related Work

Existing HPC cluster systems are built and operated in a form optimized for parallel programs, which imposes many restrictions on supporting new types of services. To overcome these rigid utilization problems and provide users with a more diverse service environment, researchers have conducted numerous studies to configure clusters using cloud virtualization technology. Virtualization technology can be divided into hypervisor-based virtualization technology and container-based virtualization technology. However, as many recent studies have shown, hypervisor-based virtualization technology inevitably results in performance degradation, whereas container-based virtualization technology is known to achieve performance close to native [5,6,11]. Consequently, researchers are conducting many studies to secure the flexibility of HPC resources by utilizing container technology in the HPC field. Notable container application technologies in the HPC field are Singularity, Shifter, and Charliecloud [3,4,9]. Singularity was specifically designed from the outset for HPC systems. Singularity [4] has a special file format (called the Singularity Image Format or SIF) to support novel features such as security, extreme portability, and guaranteed reproducibility. Shifter [3] is a prototypical implementation of container engine for HPC developed by NERSC. Shifter allow to deploy user-created images at large scale. It can support Docker images as well as several other standard image formats (vmware, ext4, squashfs, etc.) and is tied into the batch system at NERSC. CharlieCloud [9] is an open-source container technology developed by Los Alamos National Laboratory for supercomputing clusters. It uses the Linux user and mount namespaces to run industry-standard Docker containers with no privileged operations or daemons.

Recently, there has been an increase in cases of HPC operating centers running Kubernetes clusters alongside HPC clusters [2,10]. For example, the Ohio Supercomputer Center has deployed a Kubernetes cluster with tight integration to a high performance computing (HPC) environment [2,7]. Purdue University provide a composable infrastructure to launch container-based applications with Kubernetes [10]. Oak Ridge National Laboratory also operate the OpenShift environment with kubernetes [7].

3   Loosely-Coupled Integration of Kubernetes on Supercomputer

Many previous studies have attempted to integrate cloud applications with HPC systems in a tightly-coupled structure [3,4,9]. However, there are limitations due to fundamental differences between typical HPC and cloud applications. First, there are differences in how resources are utilized. Typical HPC applications require very large resources and high performance, mainly relying on exclusive resource allocation. By contrast, cloud application services mainly employ on-demand, shared resource allocation. Therefore, batch job schedulers such as PBS Pro and SLURM, widely used in HPC systems, are insufficient to meet these requirements.

Second, there are differences in the scale of tasks and service execution times. HPC applications usually execute very large-scale tasks, allocating large amounts of resources and running for very long periods. Therefore, most supercomputer operation centers set a wall-time limit to ensure fair resource usage and prevent tasks from running beyond the limit. Consequently, users must save checkpoints at regular intervals to resume their tasks from the saved point if the workload manager forcibly terminates them. By contrast, cloud applications usually involve multiple micro-services connected and executed through REST APIs. These micro-services flexibly start and stop as needed, and connections may frequently break due to various issues; hence, the service dynamically finds and connects to another micro-service. Therefore, rather than checkpoint techniques, cloud applications require methods that periodically monitor the execution status of services and dynamically create, connect, and terminate services.

Third, there are differences in the way services are executed. Performance is the most critical factor in HPC applications. To satisfy performance requirements, all compute nodes have the packages and libraries necessary for running HPC applications preinstalled, and even kernel parameters are customized. As a result, HPC applications execute jobs in batches within this optimized, closed environment. By contrast, cloud applications require a highly flexible execution approach, dynamically providing the execution environment to meet diverse user requirements. Specifically, in the cloud, rather than customizing all nodes for specific applications, flexibility is enhanced through a hypervisor layer to provide diverse application environments, even if it sacrifices performance.

Due to these fundamental dissimilarities between HPC and cloud applications, supercomputing centers operating actual systems are hesitant to adopt tightly-coupled container technologies. To address this issue, we introduce MyKSC, a loosely-coupled architecture. MyKSC is a platform that applies container technology to support the cloud-based AI and data analytics applications, which are increasing in popularity, on the supercomputer Nurion. It provides both traditional HPC applications and cloud-based applications through a unified interface. The architecture of MyKSC has three primary objectives: first, to minimize changes to existing operational HPC systems and software structures; second, to provide both HPC and cloud applications through a unified interface; and third, to enable access to the same data across all services.

Figure 1 shows the architecture of MyKSC. To provide cloud services, the entire system's resources are divided and operated between Kubernetes and traditional HPC clusters, isolating them from each other. Thus, the existing HPC cluster software remains unchanged and coexists with the Kubernetes cluster. MyKSC also controls and manages the resources of the two clusters through a web-based unified interface. It selects the appropriate cluster resources to execute applications based on the type of service that users require and delivers the results to users through a web browser. Traditional HPC applications create a job script file using the web-based interface provided by MyKSC and submit it to the batch job scheduler. The submitted job is executed through the HPC clusters, then the executed results are saved in the parallel file system. The saved results can be accessed directly allowing users to add, modify, or delete their data in MyKSC.

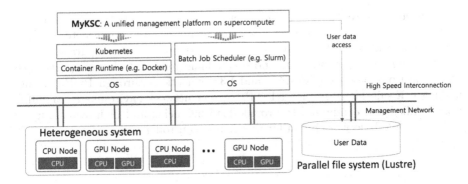

Fig. 1. Architecture of MyKSC.

On the other hand, cloud-based applications are provided in a containerized manner through a Kubernetes cluster. In MyKSC, the services provided as cloud services are jupyter, RStudio, and VNC. These applications are dynamically created through kubernetes when a user requests a service and deleted when the service is terminated.

4 Implementation

In MyKSC, the Kubernetes infrastructure is built using the software stack for cloud application services as shown in Table 1.

Table 1. MyKSC software stack

Software	Application Name	Version
OS	CentOS	7.9
Container Runtime Interface (CRI)	docker	20.10.17
CRI for GPU	nvidia-docker	2.11.0
container orchestrator	Kubernetes	1.23.9
Container Network Interface plugin	Calico	3.24.5
Service Mesh	Istio	1.15.1
Load Balancer	MetalLB	0.13.9

Kubernetes is the de facto standard framework for container orchestrators, with a rapidly growing community and ecosystem. Recently, it is also widely used in HPC systems [1,2,12]. Kubernetes consists of masters and workers, and services are executed as pods comprising one or multiple containers. In MyKSC, we chose Docker and Nvidia-docker as the container runtime interfaces. Docker is the most widely used container runtime engine, and Nvidia-docker is a container runtime engine developed by Nvidia for managing NVIDIA GPU-based containers (Docker will no longer be supported as a CRI from Kubernetes Version 1.24, and it will be replaced with cri-o or containerd in future upgrades). Calico was used for pod networking and policy management. Calico supports both L2 connections based on XVLAN and L3 connections through BGP routing, making it a suitable choice for KISTI's current network environment. MetalLB was installed and configured to provide load balancing and high availability of services, while Istio was chosen for the ingress controller.

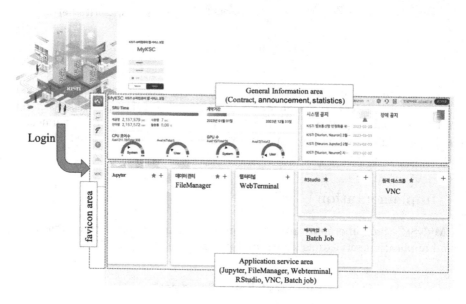

Fig. 2. MyKSC dashboard.

After logging in with a basic ID/password and two-factor authentication, users can view the dashboard shown in Fig. 2, which is the Graphical User Interface (GUI) of the implemented MyKSC. The MyKSC dashboard is divided into three sections. On the left, icons of favorites are placed for users to easily create and navigate their desired services. The top right section displays the user's contract period and remaining resources, along with statistics on Kubernetes cluster resources (CPU, Memory, GPU). The bottom right section shows the services currently provided through MyKSC, and users can create new services by clicking the "+" button. As shown in Fig. 3, created services are provided to users within the same browser frame in multiple windows.

Figure 4 shows the configuration and service creation method of MyKSC. Services are executed as pods in the Kubernetes infrastructure and created as a deployment type with three replicas for high availability and load balancing of network traffic. The created deployment connects to the outside through Istio's secure gateway, using the public IP assigned by MetalLB. SSL certificates

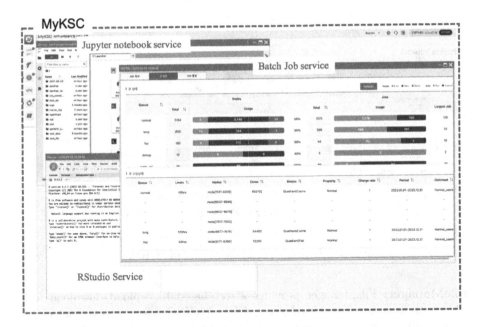

Fig. 3. The screenshot of MyKSC.

for secure communication are stored in Istio. By utilizing Istio's secure gateway, services created through MyKSC can run without an SSL certificate. In other words, users establish secure connection using the HTTPS secure protocol up to the secure gateway, and the connection between the secure gateway and the actual service uses the HTTP protocol. Also, since MyKSC does not use database, sessions cannot be shared between the created replicas. Therefore, Istio's DestinationRule fuction is used to maintain connections to the same pod for requests with a certain session.

The service creation method of MyKSC is as follows. First, when a user logs in, MyKSC retrieves the user's UID, GID, and username from LDAP and creates a namespace in the Kubernetes cluster for the logged-in user. After logging in, all Kubernetes resources created by the user are created and managed within the user's namespace. MyKSC provides a total of six services; five of them, excluding the webTerminal service that simply connects to the login node as a web terminal, are divided into the following three categories:

Jupyter, RStudio, and VNC: When a user creates Jupyter, RStudio, or VNC services, MyKSC creates pods and services through the kube-API server. When creating a pod, the "runAsUser" and "runAsGroup" values are set to the user's UID and GID values obtained from LDAP for security. These created pods are connected to clients in a sub-path format through the API Gateway implemented within MyKSC. Thus, a page requested with /jupyter connects to the Jupyter pod, and a page requested with /rstudio connects to the RStudio pod.

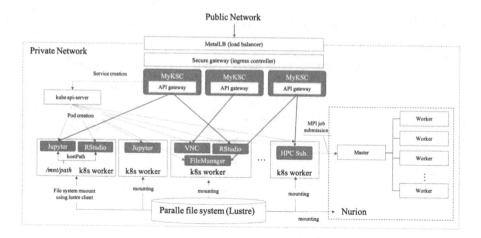

Fig. 4. The service creation process of MyKSC.

FileManager: FileManager provides a web-based file upload/download feature to manage files based on a GUI. MyKSC offers access control to two private directories provided by Nurion in the form of *hostPath* with the FileManager pod. As mentioned in Sect. 2, in Nurion, all compute nodes have the parallel file system, Lustre mounted as */home/{userName}* and */scratch/{userName}*. Therefore, when creating a FileManager pod in MyKSC, it is possible to directly access the two private directories of the parallel file system by attaching */home/{userName}* and */scratch/{userName}* as *hostPath* volume types to the FileManager pod, along with setting the "runAsUser" and "runAsGroup" values.

Batch Job: In this study, for batch job services, integration is performed in a loosely-coupled structure with the existing HPC cluster system, as presented in Sect. 3. That is, the batch job pod created in the Kubernetes cluster receives user input through a web browser and generates a job script file. The created job script file is submitted to the job scheduler's master with the user's UID, and the actual job is executed on the existing HPC cluster. However, the executed results can be verified by the user through the batch job pod.

5   Conclusion

Due to the fundamental differences between HPC application services and cloud application services, tightly-coupled integration approaches have clear restrictions, causing hesitation in their adoption by administrators. To address these challenges, this paper presented MyKSC, which provides a unified user interface based on a loosely-coupled architecture. MyKSC is applied to Nurion, a supercomputer operated by KISTI, allowing Nurion users to use new cloud application services such as Jupyter and RStudio, along with traditional HPC application services like MPI, through MyKSC.

References

1. Beltre, A.M., Saha, P., Govindaraju, M., Younge, A., Grant, R.E.: Enabling HPC workloads on cloud infrastructure using kubernetes container orchestration mechanisms. In: 2019 IEEE/ACM International Workshop on Containers and New Orchestration Paradigms for Isolated Environments in HPC (CANOPIE-HPC), pp. 11–20. IEEE (2019)
2. Dockendorf, T., Baer, T., Johnson, D.: Early experiences with tight integration of kubernetes in an HPC environment. In: Practice and Experience in Advanced Research Computing, pp. 1–4 (2022)
3. Gerhardt, L., et al.: Shifter: containers for HPC. In: Journal of physics: Conference Series, vol. 898, p. 082021. IOP Publishing (2017)
4. Godlove, D.: Singularity: simple, secure containers for compute-driven workloads. In: Proceedings of the Practice and Experience in Advanced Research Computing on Rise of the Machines (learning), pp. 1–4 (2019)
5. Kozhirbayev, Z., Sinnott, R.O.: A performance comparison of container-based technologies for the cloud. Futur. Gener. Comput. Syst. **68**, 175–182 (2017)
6. Le, E., Paz, D.: Performance analysis of applications using singularity container on SDSC comet. In: Proceedings of the Practice and Experience in Advanced Research Computing 2017 on Sustainability, Success and Impact, pp. 1–4 (2017)
7. Papadimitriou, G., Vahi, K., Kincl, J., Anantharaj, V., Deelman, E., Wells, J.: Workflow submit nodes as a service on leadership class systems. In: Practice and Experience in Advanced Research Computing, pp. 56–63 (2020)
8. Park, J.W., Hahm, J.: Container-based cluster management platform for distributed computing. In: Proceedings of the International Conference on Parallel and Distributed Processing Techniques and Applications (PDPTA), p. 34. The Steering Committee of The World Congress in Computer Science, Computer ... (2015)
9. Priedhorsky, R., Randles, T.: Charliecloud: unprivileged containers for user-defined software stacks in HPC. In: Proceedings of the International Conference for High Performance Computing, Networking, Storage and Analysis, pp. 1–10 (2017)
10. Smith, P.M., et al.: The "geddes" composable platform-an evolution of community clusters for a composable world. In: 2020 IEEE/ACM International Workshop on Interoperability of Supercomputing and Cloud Technologies (SuperCompCloud), pp. 33–38. IEEE (2020)
11. Torrez, A., Randles, T., Priedhorsky, R.: HPC container runtimes have minimal or no performance impact. In: 2019 IEEE/ACM International Workshop on Containers and New Orchestration Paradigms for Isolated Environments in HPC (CANOPIE-HPC), pp. 37–42. IEEE (2019)
12. Zhou, N., et al.: Container orchestration on HPC systems through kubernetes. J. Cloud Comput. **10**(1), 1–14 (2021)
13. Zhou, N., Zhou, H., Hoppe, D.: Containerisation for high performance computing systems: Survey and prospects. IEEE Trans. Softw. Eng. **49**, 2722–2740 (2022)

Research on Network Slicing Deployment Strategy for High Reliability Power Business Service

Jinyu Zhao[1], Lin Pang[1(✉)], Jiayi Liu[2], and Dalong Song[1]

[1] China Gridcom Co., Ltd., Shenzhen 518000, People's Republic of China
13691792028@139.com
[2] Xidian University, Xian 710000, People's Republic of China

Abstract. With the continuous advancement of smart grid construction, the flexible and ever-changing power business has higher requirements for communication networks. In this study, in order to improve the reliability of communication networks, an end-to-end network slicing backup algorithm was proposed. Firstly, the important nodes in the current network slicing were backed up to obtain a backup virtual network. The criticality of the original virtual nodes was calculated based on resources and network topology, and the deployment of highly critical virtual nodes and their corresponding backup nodes were prioritized. Then, the candidate set for each virtual node was obtained, and virtual nodes and virtual links were mapped using the Dijkstra algorithm. This algorithm backed up important nodes in the virtual network before mapping them. A link connection was made between the original virtual node and its corresponding backup virtual node, which was used to transmit its resources and information to the backup node after the original virtual node fails. The simulation results show that the algorithm effectively improves the reliability in different network scale environments.

Keywords: Smart grid · Network slicing · Reliability · Deployment strategy

1 Introduction

Reliability assessment is of great importance for power systems at different stages from design, planning to operation. Many factors threaten the reliability of the power system including aging system infrastructure, physical network problems, new forms of generation, vulnerability to climate change, etc. [1–3]. With the construction and development of smart grids, differentiated and flexible power businesses place higher demands on communication networks [4, 5].

Smart grid is one of the important applications for the 5G URLLC, where reliability and low latency are considered to be very important. Existing research on URLLC focuses on the wireless access area, which is mainly improving parameters such as packet delivery rate, BER, SNR, and outage probability to guarantee the reliability of wireless communication [6–8]. On the other hand, reliability also refers to the ability of a system or network function to provide services under various network conditions9.

Y. Zhang and L.-J. Zhang (Eds.): ICWS 2023, LNCS 14209, pp. 92–104, 2023.
https://doi.org/10.1007/978-3-031-44836-2_7

From the perspective of network slicing, the mapping reliability of Network Slicing (NS) is also manifested in the availability and functionality of virtualized network functions (vnf), which comprise the corresponding NS to ensure the service continuity of the NS. Therefore, the NS deployment problem is investigated so as to improve the reliability of the system represented by NS.

In Reference [5], the allocation of 5G core network under different vertical business environments was deeply investigated, and how to improve the utilization rate of network was the main research content. In Reference [6], the current 5G system architecture was introduced in detail, which provided sound foundation for the development and application of 5G technology. In Reference [8], the application of 5G technology in the field of smart grid and automation grid was introduced, indicating the broad application prospect of 5G technology in the field of smart grid. In Reference [9], an ultra-reliable low-latency communication algorithm was proposed, which significantly improved the communication performance of wireless networks. In References [10] and [11], network virtualization was investigated and a survivable virtual network embedding algorithm based on network virtualization was proposed. In References [12–15], the function layout, topology optimization and delay boundary of virtual mobile core network were combined to provide an important basis for the optimization of network allocation algorithms. Although the smart grid and network allocation algorithms have been investigated and p in the above articles, there is little research on reliability of the network slicing mapping. The Virtual Network Embedding (VNE) problem is further extended to the Survivable Virtual Network Embedding (SVNE) problem10. The aim is to deploy VNs in such a way that they can operate in spite of physical network failures, which is a key issue that needs to be addressed by end-users and service providers. The reliability of VNs can be improved in two ways as follows:

1) Failure avoidance, which attempts to optimize resource allocation for the deployment of VNs so that failures have as little impact as possible on the VN system.
2) Failure recovery, which attempts to provide backup resources so that the VN can still operate after being affected by a failure.

In order to address the above problems, the fault protection of virtual network nodes is mainly investigated and an S-AVNE network slicing allocation algorithm is proposed. Simulation results show that the algorithm can effectively improve the reliability of the communication network.

2 Network Slicing Resource Allocation Model

2.1 Virtual Network Model

The ITU-R defines three 5G network application scenarios [11–13]: enhanced Mobile Broad Band (eMBB), massive Machine-Type Communications (mMTC), and Ultra-Reliable and Low-Latency Communications (URLLC), with slices for each scenario having specific requirements. A virtual network is used to represent end-to-end slicing of 5G networks. The network slicing request model is represented by an undirected graph $G_O(N_O, E_O)$, where:

N_O represents a collection of virtual network functions and $n_i^O \in N_O$ represents a virtual VNF case. C_i^O represents the physical resource requirements of a virtual node n_i^O. Each virtual network node represents a virtual VNF instance, such as virtual RRU, virtual MEC server, virtual video encoder, virtual MME, and virtual gateway. E_O represents a collection of virtual links, each virtual link is represented by a $e_{ij}^O \in E_O, \forall n_i^O, n_j^O \in N_O$, B_{ij}^O represents the network bandwidth resource requirement of the virtual link e_{ij}^O. L_{ij}^O represents the transmission latency requirement of the virtual link e_{ij}^O.

2.2 Backup Virtual Network Model

Based on the topological importance of the virtual nodes and the level of resource requirements, the input of important nodes and links in the original virtual network are backed up [14–16]. If the criticality of the current virtual node is greater than the criticality thresholdS_T, a backup node with the same degree of resource demand is added and the backup node is connected to the neighboring nodes of the original virtual node. In order to transfer the resources and data from the node to the backup node in time after the node fails, a link connecting the original virtual node to the backup node is added, and a backup virtual network is obtained for mapping of the network.

Based on the metric of the virtual node importance $S(n_i^O)$, the location of important virtual nodes for extended VN backups can be determined. For a given importance threshold S_T, the virtual nodes are backed up $S(n_i^O) \geq S_T$. Then, the backup virtual network (AVN) is defined as follows:

1) The AVN is modeled by an undirected graph $G_S(N_S, E_S)$, where N_S represents the set of VNFs and E_S represents the set of virtual links.
2) N_S represents the set of virtual network functions $N_S = N_O \cup N_A, n_i^S \in N_S$ represents a virtual VNF instance. NO represents the original virtual network node collection, NA represents the backup virtual network node collection, and $S(n_i^O)$ represents the criticality of a virtual node $n_i^O \in N_O$. S represents the criticality threshold. For n_i^O of $S(n_i^O) \geq S_T$, the original virtual node, $n_i^A \in N_A$ is the corresponding backup node of the original virtual node n_i^O. C_i^S represents the physical resource requirement of the virtual node n_i^S.
3) E_S represents the set of virtual links $E_S = E_O \cup E_A$, and each original virtual link denoted by e_{ij}^S. EO represents the collection of original virtual links, EA represents the collection of backup virtual links, and each original virtual link is denoted by $e_{ij}^O \in E_O, \forall n_i^O, n_j^O \in N_O$. $E_A = E_{A1} \cup E_{A2}, E_{A1} = \{e_{ii}^A, \forall n_i^O \in N_O, n_i^A \in N_A\}$ is the set of links connecting the original virtual node to its backup node, and $E_{A2} = \{e_{ij}^A, \forall n_j^O \in \delta(n_i^O)\}$ is the set of links connected to the backup node of the original virtual node and the neighboring nodes of the original virtual node, and $e_{ij}^A \in E_A, n_i^S, n_j^S \in N_S$ represents the backup link. B_{ij}^S represents the network bandwidth resource requirement of the virtual link e_{ij}^S. L_{ij}^S represents the transmission latency requirement of the virtual link e_{ij}^S.

As shown in Fig. 1, the original virtual node n_2^O is the key node and the virtual node n_1^O and n_3^O are the neighboring nodes of the original virtual node. The backup node n_2^A

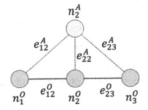

Fig. 1. Backup Virtual Network

is used to perform the backup. At the same time, the virtual links e_{12}^A and e_{23}^A are added to connect the backup node with the neighboring nodes of the original node. The virtual link e_{22}^A is added to connect the backup node with the original node, so as to make data transmit to the backup node easily when the original node fails.

2.3 Network Slicing Mapping Model

The deployment and resource allocation of network slicing lies in the mapping $M :$ $G_S \rightarrow G_I$ from the network slicing request map $G_S(N_S, E_S)$ to the physical network $G_I(N_I, E_I)$. As shown in Fig. 2, each virtual network node $n_i^S \in N_S$ is mapped to a physical entity network node $n_u^I \in N_I$ and each virtual network link e_{ij}^S is mapped to a physical network link e_{uv}^I. The problem can be described as follows: based on the physical network topology map G_I and the network slicing request graph G_S, the mapping of virtual network nodes to physical network nodes and the mapping of virtual network links to physical network links are determined, and the highest reliability of the virtual network is achieved when the constraints of virtual network latency and bandwidth requirements are satisfied [17, 18].

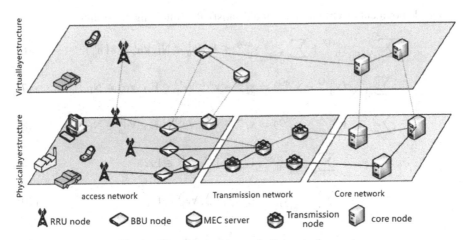

Fig. 2. 5G end-to-end network slicing deployment

In order to describe the network slicing deployment problem, two binary variables are introduced, namely x_i^{uO}, x_i^{uA}, y_{ij}^{uvO} and y_{ij}^{uvA}. $x_i^{uO} = 1$ indicates that the original virtual node n_i^O is mapped to the physical node n_u^I. $x_i^{uA} = 1$ indicates that the backup virtual node n_i^A is mapped to the physical node n_u^I. $y_{ij}^{uvO} = 1$ indicates that the original virtual link e_{ij}^O is mapped to the physical link e_{uv}^I. $y_{ij}^{uvA} = 1$ indicates that the backup virtual link e_{ij}^A is mapped to the physical link e_{uv}^I.

Each virtual node should be mapped to a physical node, and the constraint is obtained:

$$\sum\nolimits_{n_u^I \in N_I} x_i^{uO} = 1, \forall n_i^O \in N_O \tag{1}$$

$$\sum\nolimits_{n_u^I \in N_I} x_i^{uA} = 1, \forall n_i^A \in N_A \tag{2}$$

In order to ensure the security of different virtual nodes, each physical node can only map one virtual node:

$$\sum\nolimits_{n_i^A \in N_A} x_i^{uA} + \sum\nolimits_{n_i^O \in N_O} x_i^{uO} = 1, \forall n_u^I \in N_I \tag{3}$$

The sum of virtual node resource requests deployed on each physical node does not exceed the physical resources of that physical node, and the sum of virtual link bandwidth requests deployed on each physical link does not exceed the physical bandwidth resources of that physical link. Physical resource limit constraints for physical nodes:

$$\sum\nolimits_{n_i^O \in N_O} x_i^{uO} \cdot C_i^O + \sum\nolimits_{n_i^A \in N_A} x_i^{uA} \cdot C_i^A \leq C_u^I, \forall n_u^I \in N_I \tag{4}$$

Bandwidth resource limitation constraints for physical links:

$$\sum\nolimits_{e_{ij}^O \in E_O} y_{ij}^{uvO} \cdot B_{ij}^O + \sum\nolimits_{e_{ij}^A \in E_A} y_{ij}^{uvA} \cdot B_{ij}^A \leq B_{uv}^I, \forall e_{uv}^I \in E_I \tag{5}$$

The deployment of virtual links should satisfy the following constraints:

$$\sum\nolimits_{e_{ij}^O \in E_O} y_{ij}^{uvO} + \sum\nolimits_{e_{ij}^A \in E_A} y_{ij}^{uvA} \leq 1, \forall n_u^I \in N_I, \forall n_v^I \in \delta\left(n_u^I\right) \tag{6}$$

$$\sum\nolimits_{n_v^I \in N_I} (y_{ij}^{uvO} - y_{ij}^{vuO}) = x_i^{vO} - x_j^{uO}, \forall e_{ij}^O \in E_O, \forall n_u^I \in N_I \tag{7}$$

$$\sum\nolimits_{n_v^I \in N_I} (y_{ij}^{uvA} - y_{ij}^{vuA}) = x_i^{vA} - x_j^{uO}, \forall e_{ij}^O \in E_O, \forall n_u^I \in N_I \tag{8}$$

$$\sum\nolimits_{e_{uv}^I \in E_I} y_{ij}^{uvO} \cdot L_{uv}^I \leq L_{ij}^O, \forall e_{ij}^O \in E_O \tag{9}$$

$$\sum\nolimits_{e_{uv}^I \in E_I} y_{ij}^{uvA} \cdot L_{uv}^I \leq L_{ij}^A, \forall e_{ij}^A \in E_A \tag{10}$$

$$y_{ij}^{uvO} + y_{ij}^{uvA} \leq 1, \forall e_{ij}^O \in E_O, e_{uv}^I \in E_I \tag{11}$$

Link constraints ensure that physical links do not create loops, that the flow of each virtual link is conserved, that the delay of each physical link meets the delay requirements of the virtual network link, and that the original virtual link and its backup link cannot share any of the physical links. In the above equation, $\delta\left(n_u^I\right)$ is the neighbor node of the physical node n_u^I.

For grid network slicing, the reliability is its most important indicator. If we want to ensure that the reliability of network slicing is maximized, we need to ensure that the probability of failure of each link and node is minimized. In order to describe the target equation, two variables are introduced:

$$x_i^u = \begin{cases} 1 \text{ if } \sum_{n_i^S}(x_i^{uO} + x_i^{uA}) \geq 1 \\ 0 \qquad \text{Other} \end{cases} \qquad (12)$$

$$y_{ij}^{uv} = \begin{cases} 1 \text{ if } \sum_{e_{ij}^S}(y_{ij}^{uvO} + y_{ij}^{uvA}) \geq 1 \\ 0 \qquad \text{Other} \end{cases} \qquad (13)$$

When a physical node is mapped to some virtual node, $x_i^u = 1$; when a physical link is mapped to some virtual link, $y_{ij}^{uv} = 1$. Then the reliability of the network is expressed as:

$$\min 1 - \prod_{n_u^I \in N_I}\left(1 - P\left(n_u^I\right) \cdot x_i^u\right) \cdot \prod_{e_{uv}^I \in E_I}\left(1 - P\left(e_{uv}^I\right) \cdot y_{ij}^{uv}\right) \qquad (14)$$

where $P\left(n_u^I\right)$ represents the failure probability of the physical node n_u^I, and $P\left(e_{uv}^I\right)$ represents the failure probability of the physical link e_{uv}^I. In order to facilitate the calculation, the target equation is processed by log to obtain the linear target equation:

$$\max \sum_{n_u^I \in N_I} \log(1 - P(n_u^I))x_i^u - \sum_{e_{uv}^I \in E_I} \log(1 - P(e_{uv}^I)) \cdot y_{ij}^{uv} \qquad (15)$$

3   S-AVNE Network Slicing Backup Algorithm

The S-AVNE algorithm is an end-to-end network slicing backup algorithm. First, the important nodes in the current network slicing are backed up to get the backup virtual network. The node criticality of the original virtual nodes is calculated based on the resources and network topology, and the virtual nodes with high criticality and their corresponding backup nodes are prioritized. Then, for each virtual node, the candidate set is obtained, and the Dijkstra algorithm is used to map the virtual nodes and virtual links, so that the resources and information on the original virtual node can be transferred to the backup node after the failure of the original virtual node. This effectively improves the reliability of the network.

The S-AVNE algorithm can be described as follows:

S-AVNE algorithm

Input: Internet slicing request

Output: virtual network mapping results

Generate a backup virtual network, sort the nodes using a virtual node sorting algorithm, and generate a queue$N_S{'}$

for $\forall n_i^0 \in N_O$

    Calculate the criticality of each node$S(n_i^0)$

end for

Set the largest node of $S(n_i^0)$ as $\hat{n}_i^0$, with $\hat{n}_i^0$ as the root node.

Traverse the original virtual network G_O using a breadth-first search algorithm and generate a decision tree T

for each layer of T

    Sort the nodes in descending order as $S(n_i^0)$ indicator to obtain the set C

    for $n_i^0 \in C$

      Add n_i^0 into $N_S{'}$

      if $(S(n_i^0) > S_T)$

        Add n_i^A corresponding to n_i^0 into $N_S{'}$

      end if

    end for

end for

for $n_i^S \in N_S{'}$

    Use the candidate physical node set selection algorithm to obtain the candidate node set Q

    if n_i^S is the root node

      $Q = \{n_u^I | C_u^I > C_i^S\}$

    else if $n_i^S \in N_A$

      Get the physical node mapped by its corresponding original virtual node n_v^I

      Add the one-hop node of n_v^I and the physical nodes which satisfies $C_u^I > C_i^S$ into Q

    else

      Find the parent node n_p^S corresponding to this virtual node, and find the physical node n_v^I that corresponds to n_p^S.

      Add the one-hop node of n_v^I and the physical nodes which satisfies $C_u^I > C_i^S$ into Q

    end if

    if n_i^S is the root node

      Map n_i^S to the first node in Q

    else

      for $n_u^I \in Q$

        Remove links in the physical topology network whose remaining bandwidth of the link is less than the bandwidth requirement of the virtual link.

        Remove the links that have already been mapped and utilize the shortest path algorithm to get the shortest path from n_u^I to n_p^I

        if the allocation is successful, skip to step 3 and continue to allocate the next virtual node

        end if

      end for

    end if

end for

The flowchart of the S-AVNE algorithm is shown below (Fig. 3):

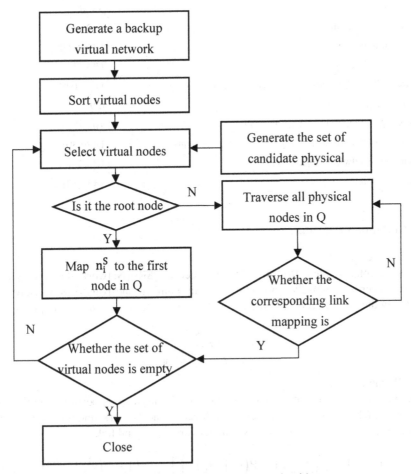

Fig. 3. The flowchart of the S-AVNE algorithm

4 Simulation of Network Slicing Deployment Algorithm

4.1 Simulation Setup Parameters

The virtual network topology of the underlying 5G physical network and network requests is generated by an improved Barabasi-Albert (BA) scale-free network model construction algorithm. The BA model is mainly used to represent the 5G system and NSR topology [17, 19, 20]. As previously described, the physical network contains access nodes (AN), transmission nodes (TN) and core nodes (CN). The ratio of these three nodes is 3:4:3. The specific parameter settings are shown in Table 1.

Table 1. Simulation Parameters

Parameters	Value
Physical node computing power	U[20,60]
Physical link bandwidth	U[200,600]
Physical link latency	U[3,5]
Failure probability of physical nodes and links	U [0, 0.05]
The default value of S_T	0.9
Number of virtual nodes per network slicing	10
Virtual network node computing resource requirements	U[20,30]
Virtual link bandwidth requirements	U[5,20]
Virtual link latency	U[30,50]

4.2 Evaluation Indicators

1) Acceptance rate

The acceptance rate is the ratio of the number of NSRs (Network Slicing Requests) that have been successfully mapped to the total number, and is used to measure how effectively the algorithm is utilizing network resources to receive service requests.

$$AR = \frac{\sum_{t=0}^{T} NUM_{acc}}{\sum_{t=0}^{T} NUM_{arr}} \tag{16}$$

2) Reliability

Reliability is an indicator measuring how well a network is performing. Network reliability can be assessed at many different levels of the network, and reliability here is calculated based on the failure of physical network nodes and links.

$$Re = 1 - \prod_{n_u^I \in N_I} \left(1 - P\left(n_u^I\right) \cdot x_i^u\right) \cdot \prod_{e_{uv}^I \in E_I} \left(1 - P\left(e_{uv}^I\right) \cdot y_{ij}^{uv}\right) \tag{17}$$

4.3 Simulation Results

In this study, four sets of simulations of the algorithm are performed. Figure 4 illustrates the relationship among the slicing acceptance rate, reliability and the number of physical nodes. The acceptance rate of S-AVNE is lower compared to the benchmark algorithm, because more physical resources are required for backing up important nodes. The reliability of NS after deployment is further calculated. Since certain $S\left(n_i^O\right)$ nodes higher than 0.9 have the same backup nodes, the reliability of S-AVNE is improved. The reliability of NS increases as the physical network expands.

Figure 5 shows the relationship among the slicing acceptance rate, reliability and the number of network slicing. The acceptance rate of S-AVNE is lower than that of

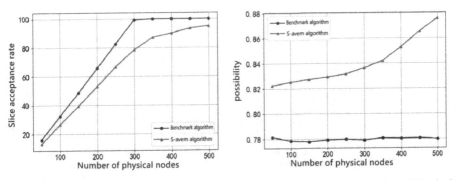

Fig. 4. The relationship among the slicing acceptance rate, reliability and the number of physical nodes

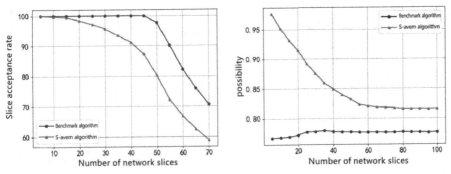

Fig. 5. The relationship among the slicing acceptance rate, reliability and the number of network slicing

the benchmark algorithm. As the number of deployed NSs increases, the reliability of S-AVNE converges to a level higher than that of the benchmark algorithm.

Figure 6 shows the relationship among the slicing acceptance rate, reliability and the number of virtual nodes. The acceptance rate of S-AVNE is lower compared to the benchmark algorithm. As the number of virtual nodes increases, S-AVNE still has higher reliability than the benchmark algorithm.

Finally, the influence of the node importance thresholds S_T is investigated. For virtual nodes with importance value $S(n_i^O)$ higher than S_T, the node should be backed up. In Fig. 4-4, it shows the acceptance rate and reliability corresponding to different S_T values. When $S_T = 0$, all virtual nodes are backed up; when $S_T = 1$, no virtual node is backed up. As the S_T value increases, the acceptance rate increases. As fewer nodes are backed up, the reliability of NS decreases (Fig. 7).

The simulation results show that AVN consumes more physical resources due to increased backup resources. However, the reliability of the NS system is greatly improved.

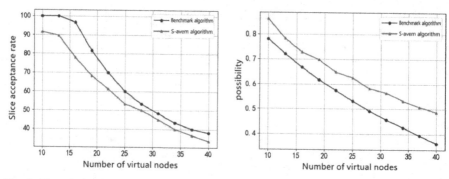

Fig. 6. The relationship among the slicing acceptance rate, reliability and the number of virtual nodes

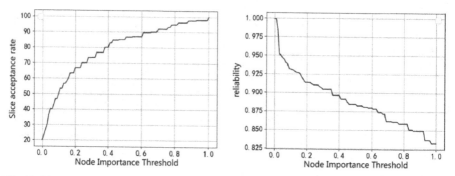

Fig. 7. The relationship among the slicing acceptance rate, reliability and importance thresholds of nodes

5   Conclusion

The reliability enhancement mechanism of NS service is investigated to solve the problem of physical network node failures. In the case of increasing number of physical nodes, the S-AVNE algorithm decreases the slice acceptance rate by 3%–5% but increases the reliability by 0.04–0.1 compared to the benchmark algorithm. When the number of network slicing increases, the S-AVNE algorithm decreases the slice acceptance rate by 0%–12% but increases the reliability by 0.1–0.21 compared to the benchmark algorithm. In the case of increasing number of virtual nodes, the S-AVNE algorithm decreases the slicing acceptance rate by 5%–9% and increases the reliability by 0.08–0.12 compared to the benchmark algorithm. At the same time, the value of the node importance threshold also has an effect on the network slicing acceptance rate and reliability. As the value of the threshold increases, the slicing acceptance rate increases by 80% but the reliability decreases by 0.17. The simulation results show that the algorithm effectively improves the reliability in different network scale environments.

References

1. Li, P., Bi, J., Yu, H., et al.: Intelligent sensing and state perception technology and application of substation equipment. J. High Volt. Technol. **46**(9), 3097–3113 (2020)
2. Ren, J., Yu, Z., Gao, G., et al.: New issues and key technologies for new power system planning under dual-carbon goals J. Power Syst. Equipmen (18), 41–42(2021)
3. Zhou, Z., Chen, Y., Pan, C., et al.: Highly reliable low-latency mobile edge computing technology for intelligent power inspection. J. High Volt. Technol. **46**(6), 1895–1902 (2020)
4. Wang, Z., Wang, Y., Mengsadula, et al.: Overview of 5G technology architecture and key technologies for power applications J. Power Inf. Commun. Technol. **18**(8), 8–19 (2020)
5. Junseok, Kim, Dongmyoung, et al.: Handover procedure considering session and service continuity mode of UE in 5G core network. In: Proceedings of Symposium of the Korean Institute of Communications and Information Sciences. Seoul, Korea: s. n. pp.129–130 (2017)
6. System architecture for the 5G system (5GS) (V16.7. 0; 3GPP TS 23.501 version 16.7. 0 release 16): ETSI TS 23 501–2021 S (2021)
7. Huang, Z., Liu, J., Li, Y.: Development status and application challenges in the first year of 5G commercialization. J. Power Inf. Commun. Technol. **18**(1), 18–25 (2020)
8. International Electrotechnical Commission. Communication networks and systems for power utility automation-part 90–4: network engineering guide lines (edition 2.0): IEC/TR 61850–90–4: 2020 S. Geneva, Switzerland: International Electrotechnical Commission (2020)
9. Popovski, P., et al.: Wireless access in ultra-reliable low latency communication (urllc). IEEE Trans. Commun. **67**(8), 5783–5801 (2019)
10. Rahman, M.R., Boutaba, R.: Svne: Survivable virtual network embedding algorithms for network virtualization. IEEE Trans. Network Serv. Manag. **10**(2), 105–118 (2013)
11. Checko, A., Christiansen, H.L., Yan, Y., et al.: Cloud RAN for mobile networks-a technology overview. J. IEEE Commun. Surv. Tutor. **17**(1), 405–426 (2015)
12. Zhu, Z., You, X., Zheng, C., Li, L., Fan, B.: A location-weighted based bandwidth estimation method for power communication sites. Wide View Oper. Technol. (2018)
13. Baumgartner, A., Reddy, V.S., Bauschert, T.: Combined virtual mobile core network function placement and topology optimization with latency bounds. In: 2015 Fourth European Workshop on Software Defined Networks, pp. 97–102. IEEE Press, Bilbao (2015)
14. Barla, I.B., Schupke, D.A., Carle, G.: Resilient virtual network design for end-to-end cloud services. In: Bestak, R., Kencl, L., Li, L.E., Widmer, J., Yin, H. (eds.) NETWORKING 2012. LNCS, vol. 7289, pp. 161–174. Springer, Heidelberg (2012). https://doi.org/10.1007/978-3-642-30045-5_13
15. Kanizo, Y., Rottenstreich, O., Segall, I., et al.: Optimizing virtual backup allocation for middleboxes. J. IEEE/ACM Trans. Networking **25**(5), 2759–2772 (2017)
16. Ibn-Khedher, H., Abd-Elrahman, E., Afifi, H.: OMAC.: optimal migration algorithm for virtual CDN C//2016 23rd International Conference on Telecommunications (ICT), Thessaloniki, pp.1–6. IEEE Press (2016)
17. Abiko, Y., Saito, T., Ikeda, D., et al.: Flexible resource block allocation to multiple slices for radio access network slicing using deep reinforcement learning. J. IEEE Access **8**, 68183–68198 (2020)
18. Vilalta, R., Muoz, R., Casellas, R., et al.: Experimental validation of resource allocation in transport network slicing using the ADRENALINE testbed. J. Photonic Network Commun. **40**(3), 82–93 (2020)

19. Martínez, R., Vilalta, R., Casellas, R., et al.: Network slicing resource allocation and moni-toring over multiple clouds and networks. In: Optical Fiber Communications Conference and Exposition (2018)

20. Qu, L., Assi, C., Shaban, K., et al.: A reliability-aware network service chain provisioning with delay guarantees in NFV-enabled enterprise datacenter networks. J. IEEE Trans. Network Serv. Manag. **14**(3), 554–568 (2017). https://doi.org/10.1109/TNSM.2017.2723090

Short Paper Track

An In-Depth Examination of Ultra-Wide Band (UWB) Pulse Duration for Accurate Localization

Somayeh Mohammady[✉][ORCID]

Technological University Dublin (TU Dublin), Dublin, Ireland
somayeh.mohammady@tudublin.ie

Abstract. This research investigates the effect of Ultra-Wide Band (UWB) pulse duration on accurate localization in positioning systems. Through comprehensive analysis and simulations, we explore the trade-offs between pulse duration, localization accuracy, and tracking speed, specifically focusing on Time-of-Arrival (TOA)-based positioning. The study sheds light on how different pulse durations influence time resolution, signal-to-noise ratio (SNR), and the system's ability to track dynamic movements. Our findings offer valuable insights to guide the selection of optimal pulse durations for precise localization in a variety of practical applications, striking the right balance between accuracy and real-time tracking.

Keywords: Ultra-Wide Band (UWB) · power efficiency · IoT applications · Time-of-Arrival (TOA) · satellite communications · signal-to-noise ratio (SNR

1 Introduction

1.1 Background of Ultra Wide Band (UWB) Signal

Ultra-Wide Band (UWB) technology has gained significant attention in recent years due to its potential to revolutionize various industries, especially in the Internet of Things (IoT) domain. UWB signals offer a unique combination of high data rates, precise localization capabilities, and low power consumption, making them ideal for a wide range of IoT applications [7]. However, to fully realize their potential, improvements in power efficiency are necessary. In this article, we delve into the history of UWB technology, explore existing products and services, and discuss several aspects of how power efficiency can be improved to make UWB signals more suitable for IoT applications. The history of UWB technology goes back to early 20th-century, when Heinrich Hertz and Guglielmo Marconi experienced UWB for wireless communication [9]. UWB was not widely used until the 1960s when researchers began exploring its applications in military communications such as radars. Later in the 1990s, a wide spectrum for

Supported by organization x.

unlicensed UWB use was allocated by the Federal Communications Commission (FCC), which lead to a surge in relevant researches and industrial and commercial development [2]. UWB started to receive more attraction in 2000 s with applications in IoT sectors. Various companies have incorporated the UWB technology into their products and services. Some of the well known products are Apple's U1 Chip uses UWB for spatial awareness and precise indoor positioning [3], vehicle tracking and short range communication's application in automotive application [10], and Pet tracking in smart home applications [4].

2   Frequency Comparison of GPS, Bluetooth, and UWB Technologies

Global Positioning System (GPS), Bluetooth, and UWB are all wireless communication technologies that operate at different frequency ranges. A comparison is illustrated in Fig. 1, which shows that the GPS operates mainly in around 1.6 GHz and secondly in around 1.2 GHz. These microwave range frequencies are allocated for satellite navigation systems and are relatively low compared to some other wireless technologies. GPS signals are primarily used for accurate positioning, navigation, and timing across various applications such as mapping, vehicle tracking, and outdoor location-based services.

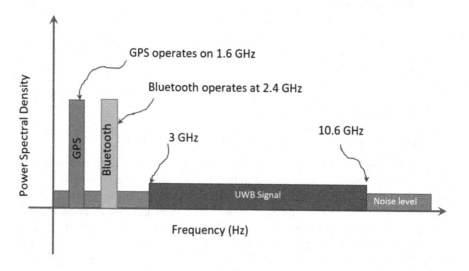

Fig. 1. Comparison of UWB versus GPS, and Bluetooth

It is seen on Fig. 1 that the Bluetooth technology operates within the 2.4 GHz Industrial, Scientific, and Medical (ISM) band. Specifically, it uses frequencies between 2.402 GHz and 2.480 GHz. This frequency range is widely used for various wireless communication technologies due to its unlicensed nature. Bluetooth offers short-range wireless connectivity for devices such as smartphones, laptops, headphones, and smart home devices. Its frequency band is shared with other wireless technologies, which can sometimes lead to interference and congestion in crowded areas.

The UWB operates at a much higher frequency range compared to GPS and Bluetooth. It leverages a wide spectrum of frequencies spanning from 3.1 GHz to 10.6 GHz, which is significantly broader than the frequency ranges of GPS and Bluetooth. UWB pulses have very short durations, allowing them to occupy such a wide bandwidth. UWB's unique frequency range enables high data rates, precise localization, and robustness against interference. It's suitable for applications requiring accurate indoor positioning, high-data-rate communication, and ranging [18].

In summary, GPS operates in the microwave range at L1 and L2 frequencies, Bluetooth operates in the 2.4 GHz ISM band, and UWB spans a wide frequency range from 3.1 GHz to 10.6 GHz. The choice of frequency range for each technology is driven by factors such as signal propagation, interference considerations, regulatory constraints, and the specific use cases they are designed to address.

2.1   Characteristics of Ultra-Wide Band (UWB) Signals

A UWB pulse signal is Visualized in Fig. 2. The pulse is centered at 2.5GHz with a Gaussian shape and a duration of 100 ns. Time domain signal is shown in the Fig. 2(a) which exhibits the Gaussian pulse shape with fast rise and fall times. It can be seen that the signal's duration is very short and this enables high data rates and precise localization.

Frequency spectrum of the UWB pulse using the fast Fourier transform (FFT) is shown in Fig. 2(b). As expected, the UWB pulse exhibits a wide frequency spectrum, spanning over a large bandwidth due to its short pulse duration. As a result, high data rate and robustness against multi-path interference can be achieved by UWB signal. Moreover, wide bandwidth makes the power usage more efficient and makes it suitable for various IoT applications, such as satellite communications, and aerospace.

3   Precision Positioning with Ultra-Wide Band (UWB)

The Ultra-Wide Band (UWB) signal's short duration, allows for high data rates and precise localization. A basic UWB pulse with a Gaussian shape and duration of T seconds can be expressed by Eq. 1:

$$u(t) = \exp\left(-\pi\left(\frac{t}{T}\right)^2\right) \qquad (1)$$

where t represents time, and T is the duration of the pulse. In the other hand, the bandwidth of a UWB signal which is defined as the range of frequencies over which the signal's energy can be considered significant can be represented by (B),

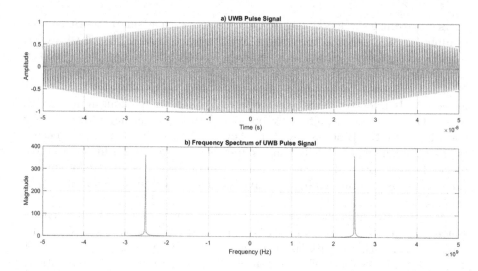

Fig. 2. UWB Pulse with Gaussian shape at 2.5 GHz

and for a Gaussian-shaped UWB pulse, the bandwidth (B) can be calculated in time domain using the expression as follows:

$$B = \frac{0.35}{T} \tag{2}$$

The constant factor 0.35 in Eq. 2 is approximately equal to $\frac{1}{2\pi}$. The constant factor 0.35 is approximately equal to $\frac{1}{2\pi}$ and it is due to the Gaussian function and its Fourier transform. A Gaussian function in the time domain is given by:

$$u(t) = \exp\left(-\pi \left(\frac{t}{T}\right)^2\right) \tag{3}$$

The Fourier transform of this Gaussian function generates a Gaussian function in the frequency domain. The standard deviation (σ) of the frequency domain Gaussian function is inversely proportional to the standard deviation of the time-domain Gaussian pulse, which is related to the pulse duration (T) as:

$$\sigma = \frac{1}{2\pi T} \tag{4}$$

The bandwidth (B) of a Gaussian-shaped pulse can be considered as the range of frequencies where the Fourier transform of the pulse is non-zero, i.e., within $\pm\sigma$. Therefore, the bandwidth (B) is given by:

$$B = 2\sigma = \frac{1}{\pi T} \tag{5}$$

The B can be expressed in terms of 0.35 instead of π as $B = \frac{0.35}{T}$. This approximation simplifies the expression for bandwidth, and it is quite close to the actual value of $\frac{1}{2\pi}$. More precisely, $0.35 \approx \frac{1}{2\pi}$. Thus, the constant factor 0.35 in the expression for bandwidth reflects the relationship between the pulse duration (T) and the bandwidth (B) in Gaussian-shaped UWB signals. Therefore, the constant factor 0.35 is approximately equal to $\frac{1}{2\pi}$ due to the mathematical properties of the Gaussian function and its Fourier transform. This approximation simplifies the expression for bandwidth and highlights the inverse relationship between pulse duration and bandwidth in UWB signals. Moreover, from this equation, it can be observed that as the duration T decreases, the bandwidth B increases proportionally. In other words, the shorter the pulse duration, the wider the bandwidth of the UWB signal. As discussed earlier, the UWB signal has a wide bandwidth, i.e. 3 GHz as shown in the simulated plot in Fig. 2, which used a Gaussian pulse shape with a duration of $T = 100$ ns. The bandwidth (B) can be calculated using $B = \frac{0.35}{T}$. Substituting the value of $T = 100$ ns (or $T = 100 \times 10^{-9}$ seconds) into the equation $B = \frac{0.35}{100 \times 10^{-9}} = 3.5 \times 10^9 \, Hz$, the bandwidth of the simulated UWB signal is calculated to be approximately 3.5 GHz. This range of bandwidth enables UWB to transmit data at high rates, as the Shannon-Hartley theorem [8] states that the maximum data rate (R) that can be achieved over a communication channel is:

$$R = B. \log_2(1 + SNR) \tag{6}$$

where the SNR is the signal-to-noise ratio. With UWB's wide bandwidth, the channel capacity [$\log_2(1 + SNR)$] increases, allowing for higher data rates compared to narrow-band systems. The relationship between the Ultra-Wide Band (UWB) signal's bandwidth, its duration, data rate, and range is analyzed and the following figures are presented to visualize these relationships. Figure 3 illustrates the bandwidth and data rate changes with UWB signal's duration.

As it can be seen on Fig. 3(a), as the pulse duration decreases (T), the bandwidth (B) increases. This inverse relationship aligns with the theoretical expression $B = \frac{0.35}{T}$ for a Gaussian-shaped UWB pulse, where 0.35 is approximately equal to $\frac{1}{2\pi}$. Hence, shorter pulse durations result in wider bandwidths, which is a desirable characteristic for achieving high data rates. This effect is illustrated by Fig. 3(b). A fixed signal-to-noise ratio (SNR) of 10 dB is used in order to calculate the data rate based on the Shannon-Hartley theorem. This is due to the fact that in wireless communication, the SNR signifies the balance between the strength of the desired signal and the level of background noise and interference. In the context of the Shannon-Hartley theorem, a standardized SNR value, often set at 10 dB, is employed to calculate data rates.

This fixed SNR value acts as a practical reference for analyzing communication system performance, facilitating straightforward comparisons across various technologies. The choice of 10 dB simplifies calculations and offers a common ground for evaluation.

For instance, in the Shannon-Hartley theorem, which relates channel capacity C to bandwidth B and SNR SNR, so we can see that $C = B \cdot \log_2(1 + SNR)$, where C denotes capacity in bits per second and B represents bandwidth in hertz, the utilization of an SNR of 10 dB results in a clear numerical outcome. Decibels dB represent a logarithmic scale that conveniently condenses a wide range of values into a comprehensible format.

By incorporating an SNR of 10 dB in data rate calculations, the relationship between bandwidth and data transmission capacity becomes lucid. While actual SNR values in real-world scenarios can vary, this standardized reference value serves as a valuable comparative tool, illustrating the influence of different bandwidths on data rates under typical signal-to-noise circumstances.

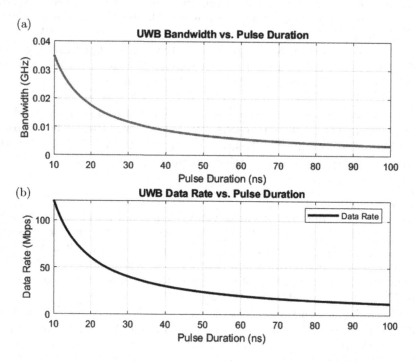

Fig. 3. a) UWB Bandwidth vs. Pulse Duration, b) UWB Data Rate vs. Pulse Duration

Operating Ultra-Wide Band (UWB) signals close to the noise level offers a range of strategic advantages in wireless communication. By utilizing UWB's wide frequency spectrum and low power spectral density, this approach optimizes spectrum utilization and enhances coexistence with other signals. UWB's innate resistance to narrowband interference is particularly potent in this configuration, ensuring robust data transmission in noisy environments. Moreover, operating UWB near the noise floor amplifies its security profile, as its low probability of detection hinders unauthorized signal interception. This strategy aligns with energy efficiency goals, as UWB's thin spread of energy across the spectrum reduces its impact on noise levels for other communication systems. Additionally, regulatory compliance is more easily maintained. Altogether, this methodology harnesses UWB's distinctive traits to achieve resilient and efficient wireless communication.

It should be noted that UWB signals are uniquely set apart from noise by their distinct characteristics. With their wide frequency spectrum distribution and low power spectral density, UWB signals exhibit a spread of energy across frequencies, enabling easy differentiation from the more concentrated and unstructured nature of noise. Their utilization of extremely short pulses, often in the nanosecond range, facilitates precise temporal patterns that stand out against noise. This, coupled with their exceptional time resolution, allows for accurate time-of-arrival measurements. UWB signals also benefit from a favorable Signal-to-Noise Ratio (SNR) due to their wide bandwidth and low power density, ensuring clear distinction from background noise. UWB's compliance with regulatory frameworks further ensures its differentiation from other electromagnetic emissions. Collectively, these distinctive attributes empower UWB signals to effectively and reliably overcome the challenges posed by noise, making them well-suited for applications demanding accurate positioning, high data rates, and robust communication in complex wireless environments. The range of UWB is also analyzed by varying the pulse duration (T), and using time-of-arrival (TOA) method.

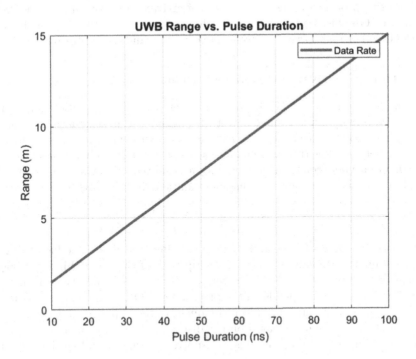

Fig. 4. UWB Range vs. Pulse Duration

Figure 4 shows as the pulse duration increases, the range also increases, as the longer pulse allows for more accurate time-of-arrival measurements. This is because a longer pulse provides a better-defined signal presence, making it easier for the receiver to precisely determine when the pulse arrived. Shorter pulses with rapid rise and fall times can lead to timing uncertainties, resulting in less accurate TOA measurements. In essence, longer pulses offer higher time resolution, enhancing the receiver's ability to pinpoint the exact arrival time of the signal. This accuracy directly improves distance calculation and localization precision, essential for reliable positioning systems.

This direct relationship indicates that by achieving high data rate, the UWB signal is capable of reaching further distance as desired in many long distance IoT applications. High bandwidth and high data rate makes UWB signals well-suited for real-time communication, fast tracking applications in IoT devices. The short and rapid pulse allows for highly accurate time-of-arrival (TOA) measurements, making it ideal for precise localization and indoor positioning of IoT applications such as indoor trackings and healthcare applications.

4   UWB Tracking and Positioning

The tracking process is done through time-of-arrival (TOA) or time-difference-of-arrival (TDOA) measurements [11], which involves determining the time it takes for the UWB signal to travel between a transmitter and receiver or receivers [12].

4.1   Time-of-Arrival (TOA) Localization

In TOA localization, the UWB transmitter emits a short-duration pulse, and UWB receivers within the range detect the transmitted pulse [13]. Each receiver records the time at which it received the pulse with high precision [14]. The distance between the transmitter and each receiver is calculated based on the time difference between the transmission time and reception time [11]. Using the speed of light as a constant, the distance can be determined as:

$$Distance = \frac{c \times TOA}{2} \tag{7}$$

where c is the speed of light and TOA is the time-of-arrival. The factor of 2 in the denominator accounts for the round-trip time of the signal. Since the speed of light is constant ($c \approx 3 \times 10^8$ meters per second), the accuracy of distance measurements mainly depends on the precision of TOA measurements. Trilateration (2D) or multilateration (3D) techniques are then applied to determine the position of the transmitter based on the distances from three or more receivers [15]. For example if a UWB pulse is transmitted at time t_t and received at time t_r. The TOA, is calculated by $t = t_r - t_t$.

4.2   Time-Difference-of-Arrival (TDOA) Localization

TDOA localization requires at least two UWB receivers to detect the transmitted pulse [19]. Each receiver records the time at which it received the pulse, similar to TOA [13]. The time difference between the arrivals of the pulse at different receivers, known as TDOA, is then calculated [16]. Using the speed of light, the difference in distances between the transmitter and the two receivers can be determined based on the TDOA:

$$\Delta Distance = \frac{c \times TDOA}{2} \tag{8}$$

multilateration techniques together with the TDOA from multiple receiver pairs, determines the position of the transmitter in 2D or 3D space [11]. In TDOA localization, multiple UWB receivers are used to detect the same UWB pulse transmitted by a single UWB transmitter. The TDOA between the arrivals of the pulse at different receivers is measured. For example if two receivers, R_1 and R_2 are considered, the pulse is received at times t_{r_1} and t_{r_2}, respectively, therefore, the TDOA, is calculated by $t_{12} = t_{r_1} - t_{r_2}$. By combining the TDOA measurements from multiple receivers, the location of the transmitter can be determined using multilateration techniques, such as the intersection of hyperbolas or spheres corresponding to the measured TDOAs.

4.3   Real Time Tracking and Accuracy

To achieve real-time tracking, specially when the object or person is moving, the UWB system can continually update the position of the transmitter based on new TOA or TDOA measurements received from the UWB receivers [17]. The accuracy of UWB-based localization depends on several factors, including the synchronization accuracy between transmitter and receivers, multipath effects, and resolution of TOA/TDOA measurements. UWB localization is known for its high accuracy, and in clear line-of-sight environments, With precise timing and synchronization techniques, UWB localization can achieve centimeter-level accuracy. However, in a complex indoor environments with multipath reflections, the accuracy may degrade as the signal suffers from interference and reflections.

4.4   The Impact of Pulse Duration on Tracking

There is a trade-off between localization accuracy and tracking speed. The pulse duration directly influences the Time-of-Arrival (TOA) or Time-Difference-of-Arrival (TDOA) measurements, which are essential for accurate localization in UWB systems. Shorter pulses provide better time resolution, enabling more precise TOA or TDOA measurements. This results in higher localization accuracy, especially in environments with multipath reflections and noise. In the other hand, shorter pulses reduce the energy per pulse, which can lead to weaker received signal strength at the receivers.

This can affect the tracking speed as the system may require more pulses to achieve a reliable tracking update. Longer pulses, while providing more energy and better tracking performance, might reduce the localization accuracy due to lower time resolution. The effect of Pulse Duration on Localization Accuracy and Tracking Speed are analyzed and the results are visualized in the Fig. 5. It is observed from Fig. 5(a) that localization accuracy changes with varying pulse durations, and as the pulse duration decreases, better time resolution is achieved and therefore the localization accuracy improves. Figure 5(b) displays the relationship between the tracking speed and different pulse durations. It is observed that as the pulse duration decreases, shorter pulses allow for more frequent updates, and it results in better tracking speed. This analysis helps in understanding the trade-offs between localization accuracy and tracking speed in UWB positioning systems and can guide the selection of an appropriate pulse duration for a specific application's requirements.

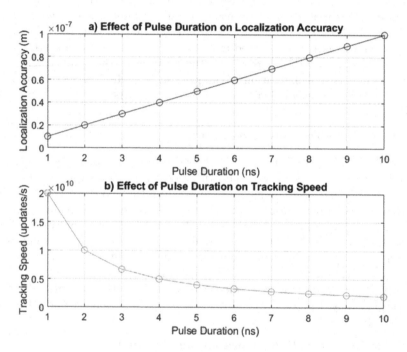

Fig. 5. a) Effect of Pulse Duration on Localization Accuracy, b) Effect of Pulse Duration on Tracking Speed

5   Factors Influencing UWB Localization Accuracy

Signal propagation, interference, and environmental conditions play crucial roles in influencing the performance of Ultra-Wide Band (UWB) localization and its accuracy. Here's a detailed explanation of their impacts:

– UWB signals are known by their wide bandwidth, which makes them strong to multi-path propagation. However, certain signal propagation phenomena can still affect them. For example, Reflections can introduce delays in the signal arrival. In indoor environments, UWB signals can reflect off walls, floors, and objects. The delays in the signal arrival, leads to errors in time-of-arrival (TOA), which may degrade localization accuracy, if not compensated. Multipath Fading may occur due to bouncing and reflections and makes the signal to take multiple paths to reach the receiver. From signal processing point of view, the constructive and/or destructive interference of various paths can result in fluctuations in signal strength, affecting the accuracy of the measured distance.

– Another phenomena is known as interference of signals from other wireless devices and electronic signals operating in the same or close frequency range that can disrupt UWB communication and localization. The interference can add extra noise to the received signal which leads to inaccurate time measurement. This can result in errors in TOA or time-difference-of-arrival (TDOA) calculations and subsequently impact the localization. Moreover data can get corrupted due to interference which leads to loss of data and errors in the transmitted information, therefore, the acuracy of the position may degrade.

– Additionally, environmental Conditions in which UWB systems operate can also impact their localization accuracy. For example physical obstructions such as walls, obstacles, and furniture can reflect of block the UWB pulses. This can lead to signal delays, attenuation, and changes in signal propagation paths, affecting the accuracy. Moreover,it should be noted that in ideal Line of Sight (LOS) scenarios, where there is a direct and unobstructed path between the transmitter and receiver, UWB accuracy can be higher. In Non-Line-of-Sight (NLOS) scenarios, where there are obstacles or reflections, accuracy may decrease due to complex signal paths. Changes in the environment, such as moving objects or changing layouts, can also affect UWB signal propagation and accuracy. Therefore, a dynamic environment requires an adaptive algorithm to maintain accurate localization. The noise from environment such as electromagnetic interference from other devices transmitting nearby, can affect the accuracy of the UWB system's sensors and transceivers and it is necessary to consider employing filters to mitigate the impact of noise on accuracy.

The impacts of signal propagation, interference, and environmental conditions on UWB localization accuracy indicates the need for sophisticated algorithms, signal processing techniques, and hardware design to minimize these effects. Therefore, error correction methods, adaptive algorithms, and careful calibration are generally fundamental features of a UWB system in order to ensure accurate and reliable localization in various operating conditions.

6   Future Works

The integration of UWB technology into the Internet of Things (IoT) heralds a new era of innovation. Drawing from the extensive discussions on UWB's attributes, power efficiency enhancements, and their implications for IoT landscapes, the horizon is rife with exciting prospects and untapped potential across diverse domains. Such as:

- UWB's Trailblazing Path: UWB technology's trajectory is marked by relentless progress. Ongoing research seeks to enhance hardware, algorithms, and protocols. Advancements include sophisticated UWB transceivers, tailored waveform designs, and robust error mitigation tactics combating interference and attenuation. The synergy between academia and industry is set to yield breakthroughs, elevating performance and expanding UWB's adoption.
- Elevating Precision in Localization: The pursuit of pinpoint accuracy persists, poised to transition UWB into fusion-driven strategies. Collaborations with sensor fusion, Wi-Fi, and Bluetooth will heighten accuracy in complex environments. Dynamic adaptive algorithms are anticipated, recalibrating UWB parameters contextually to maintain robustness amid signal propagation challenges.
- UWB's Dance with Mobility and Tracking: The integration of UWB into real-time tracking systems promises a symphony of possibilities. Novel tracking algorithms are set to empower UWB with seamless updates on mobile entities and individuals. This advancement holds profound implications for scenarios ranging from industrial asset tracking to seamless navigation within healthcare and retail domains.
- UWB as a Sentinel of Security and Privacy: UWB's distinctive attributes also open the gateway to fortified communication security and individual privacy in the IoT arena. Future endeavors will delve into encryption techniques and authentication protocols specially curated for UWB signals, creating an impregnable fortress for data integrity and user confidentiality within UWB-enabled ecosystems.
- Breathing Life into Ultra-Low Power IoT Devices: Energy efficiency remains a cornerstone of IoT architecture. Future trajectories envision a further reduction in UWB-powered device energy consumption, ensuring extended battery longevity for wearables, smart sensors, and remote monitoring instruments.
- The Marriage of UWB with 5G and Beyond: The synergy between UWB and the cascading waves of 5G and its successors is poised for exploration. The harmonious integration with 5G networks is projected to fortify UWB's range and reliability, broadening its vistas beyond short-range scenarios.
- Navigating Regulation and Standardization: As UWB sets sail, the currents of regulation and standardization merit careful navigation. Future inquiries will unravel regulatory intricacies, champion spectrum accessibility, and contribute to standardization endeavors that pave the way for a seamless global embrace of UWB.
- Uncharted Research Horizons: Emerging research frontiers beckon. The aerospace sector holds great promise, with UWB poised to revolutionize satellite communication, navigation, and surveillance systems. Moreover, as safeguarding becomes paramount, UWB's security virtues can fortify critical infrastructure with resilient and secure connectivity.

UWB technology's narrative unfolds dramatically in aerospace and safeguard applications. In aviation and satellite systems, UWB reshapes navigation, communication, and tracking, while its security attributes fortify critical infrastructure with resilient connectivity. This unfolding saga marks an era where UWB orchestrates a symphony of accuracy, efficiency, and connectivity, weaving seamlessly into IoT and beyond. With vast research potential, these frontiers promise transformative discoveries that will shape UWB's next evolutionary phase.

7 Conclusion

This research extensively investigates the impact of Ultra-Wide Band (UWB) pulse duration on precise localization in positioning systems. Through comprehensive analysis and simulations, the trade-offs between pulse duration, localization accuracy, and tracking speed has been explored with a specific focus on Time-of-Arrival (TOA) and Time-Difference-of-Arrival (TDOA) methods. We observe that shorter pulses offer improved time resolution, leading to higher localization accuracy, while longer pulses enhance tracking speed by providing more energy. The results contribute significantly to understanding the balance between localization accuracy and tracking speed in UWB positioning systems, assisting in the selection of an appropriate pulse duration tailored to the specific requirements of each application. This research provides valuable knowledge to advance the application of UWB technology in various domains, including IoT, satellite communications, aerospace, and healthcare.

Acknowledgement. This publication has emanated from research conducted with the financial support of Science Foundation Ireland (SFI) under Grant Number 13/RC/2077_P2.

References

1. Dardari, D., Decarli, N., Decarli, M.: Ultra-Wideband Radar Sensing: Theory and Applications. CRC Press (2019)
2. Federal Communications Commission (FCC). Ultra-Wideband (UWB) Technology (2021). https://www.fcc.gov/engineering-technology/policy-and-rules-division/general/unlicensed-devices/ultra-wideband-uwb-technology
3. Apple Inc. U1- Chip Ultra-Wideband Technology Overview (2021). https://developer.apple.com/documentation/uikit/u1chip
4. Dardari, D., Conti, A., Ferner, U., Giorgetti, A., Win, M.Z., Zanier, M.: Ranging with ultrawide bandwidth signals in multipath environments. Proc. IEEE **101**(6), 1390–1402 (2013)
5. Kim, J., Kim, K.: Power-efficient ultra-wideband communication systems. IEEE Trans. Circuits Syst. I Regul. Pap. **67**(2), 610–623 (2020)
6. Khatun, S., Islam, S.M., Hossain, M.S., Islam, M.T.: Energy harvesting and transfer for next-generation wireless communications: a comprehensive survey. IEEE Access **9**, 78913–78930 (2021)
7. Dardari, D., Decarli, N., Decarli, M.: Ultra-Wideband Radar Sensing: Theory and Applications. CRC Press (2019)

8. Gragido, W., Pirc, J., Selby, N., Molina, D.: Chapter 4 - signal-to-noise ratio. In: Gragido, W., Pirc, J., Selby, N., Molina, D. (eds.) Blackhatonomics, Syngress, pp. 45–55 (2013). https://doi.org/10.1016/B978-1-59-749740-4.00004-6. ISBN 9781597497404

9. Hertz, H., Marconi, G.: UWB technology: Early 20th-century experiments in wireless communication, Journal of Wireless Communication History

10. Kocks, C.: A localization and tracking application for UWB. In: 2nd International Symposium on Applied Sciences in Biomedical and Communication Technologies, Bratislava, Slovakia 2009, pp. 1–5 (2009). https://doi.org/10.1109/ISABEL.2009.5373696

11. Liu, C., Pan, C., Wei, T., Wu, Y.: Ultra-wideband positioning and its applications. IEEE Trans. Industr. Electron. **67**(5), 3911–3921 (2020)

12. Huang, Y., Gao, F.: Principles and challenges of ultra-wideband technology in wireless sensor networks. Int. J. Distrib. Sens. Netw. **16**(3), 1550147720910455 (2020)

13. Alshbatat, A.M., Abu Tarboush, H.F.: A survey on localization algorithms in wireless sensor networks. Int. J. Distrib. Sens. Netw. **13**(3), 1550147717699203 (2017)

14. He, M., Xiao, B., Wang, Z., Shen, L.: Time synchronization for ultra-wideband-based wireless sensor networks. IEEE Trans. Industr. Inf. **15**(1), 341–350 (2019)

15. Rahman, S.M.M., Khan, M.F.M., Rahman, M.T.: Performance evaluation of time of arrival (TOA) and time difference of arrival (TDOA) based localization techniques for wireless sensor networks. J. Commun. Networks **22**(1), 50–57 (2020)

16. Thomas, J.L., Veen, A.J.V., Molisch, A.F.: Ultra-wideband indoor positioning systems: a comparative survey. IEEE Commun. Surv. Tutorials **21**(1), 16–34 (2019)

17. Mo, L., Yiu, S.M., Mamoulis, N.: Accurate and efficient range-based indoor localization. IEEE Trans. Mob. Comput. **15**(5), 1201–1214 (2016)

18. Inpixon: Ultra-Wideband (UWB) Technology. https://www.inpixon.com/technology/standards/ultra-wideband

19. Huynh, T., Brennan, C.: Efficient UWB indoor localization using ray-tracing propagation. In: 9th IT and T Conference, School of Computer Sciences, Technological University Dublin (2009)

Author Index

A
Anh, N. T.   32, 47

B
Bang, L. K.   32, 47
Bao, Q. T.   32, 47

C
Chen, Peng   3
Chen, Xiaofan   65
Chen, Zihong   65

H
Hien, Q. N.   32, 47
Hieu, M. D.   32, 47
Hong, K. V.   32, 47
Hong, Taeyoung   83
Huong, H. L.   47

K
Khiem, H. G.   32, 47
Khoa, T. D.   32, 47

L
Li, Fan   3
Li, Jinpeng   3
Li, Yin   3
Liu, Bozhong   65
Liu, Hui   3
Liu, Jiayi   92
Loc, V. C. P.   32, 47
Luong, H. H.   32

M
Mohammady, Somayeh   107

N
Nam, T. B.   32, 47
Ngan, N. T. K.   32, 47

P
Pang, Lin   92
Park, Ju-Won   83
Phuc, N. T.   32, 47

Q
Quy, T. L.   32, 47

S
Son, H.   32, 47
Song, Dalong   92
Syu, Yang   18

T
Triet, M. N.   32, 47
Trong, D. P. N.   32, 47

W
Wang, Chien-Min   18
Woo, Joon   83

X
Xia, Yunni   3
Xu, Chengzhong   65

Y
Ye, Kejiang   65
Yi, Jia   65
Yu, Xian   65

Z
Zeng, Feng   3
Zhao, Jiale   3
Zhao, Jinyu   92

© The Editor(s) (if applicable) and The Author(s), under exclusive license
to Springer Nature Switzerland AG 2023
Y. Zhang and L.-J. Zhang (Eds.): ICWS 2023, LNCS 14209, p. 121, 2023.
https://doi.org/10.1007/978-3-031-44836-2

Printed in the United States
by Baker & Taylor Publisher Services